TWENTIETH CENTURY

DESIGN
CLASSICS

TWENTIETH CENTURY
DESIGN CLASSICS

CHRIS PEARCE

BLOSSOM

AN H. C. BLOSSOM BOOK

ISBN 1 872532 32 2

DESIGN   DAVID GOODMAN

EDITOR   JANITA CLAMP

TYPESET   IN GREAT BRITAIN BY CAMBRIAN TYPESETTERS

PRINTED AND BOUND IN HONG KONG

A CATALOGUE RECORD FOR THIS BOOK IS AVAILABLE FROM THE BRITISH LIBRARY

H.C. BLOSSOM
6/7 WARREN MEWS
LONDON   W1P 5DJ

*The author and publishers would like to thank the following for their
help in the production of this book:*

AGA Aga-Rayburn, Shropshire, England (p 13): AIRSTREAM TRAILER
Airstream Inc, Ohio, (p 15); THE BARCELONA CHAIR Knoll International,
Shropshire (p 20); BEL GEDDES AIRLINER NUMBER 4 by permission of
the executrix Mrs Edith Lutyens Bel Geddes and Hoblitzelle Theatre Arts
Library, The Humanities Research Centre, University of Texas (p 24):
CITROEN 2CV Nicky Wright/The National Motor Museum, Beaulieu
(p 31); COCA-COLA Coca-Cola Great Britain, London (front cover, p 32);
COLDSPOT REFRIGERATOR by kind permission of Mrs Viola Loewy,
and URLA, Paris and Internationales Design Zentrum, Berlin (p 35);
CONCORD POWERFLOOD Concord Lighting Limited, London (p 37);
DESOUTTER ELECTRIC DRILLS Peter Tobitt of the Desoutter Group
(p 38); ERICOFON Design Museum (p 43); FALCON PIPE G. Smith &
Sons, The Snuff Centre, London (p 45); FENDER STRATOCASTER Rick
and Marty at Vintage and Rare Guitars, London (p 46); JEEP The
National Motor Museum, Beaulieu (p 55); THE LAND CAMERA Kate
Rouse, The Royal Photographic Society, Bath (p 8, p 58); LONDON
TRANSPORT Sheila Taylor and Tricia Austin, London Transport
Museum (p 61, p 62, p 63, p 64, p 65); McDONALD'S McDonald's
Restaurants Limited (p 10, p 68, p 69); THE MINI The Motoring Picture
Library, Beaulieu (p 71); MINOX CAMERA Kate Rouse, The Royal
Photographic Society, Bath (p 73); MOKA EXPRESS COFFEE JUG
Algerian Coffee Stores Ltd, London (p 6, p 75); MOULTON BICYCLE The
Design Museum (p 77); OLIVETTI LETTERA 22 The Design Museum
(p 79); PARKER 51 I. F. Wayman of Parker Pens (UK) Ltd (p 82);
PENGUIN POOL AT LONDON ZOO Valerie Bennett, The Architectural
Association (p 88, p 89); THE RIETVELD CHAIR 1917, Gerrit Rietveld,
copyright DACS 1991, Stedelijk Museum, Amsterdam, Holland (p 91);
ROLADEX 5024 Astrohome, London (p 93); ROSENTHAL STUDIO LINE
2000 by kind permission of Mrs Viola Loewy, and Rosenthal AG,
Selb/Germany and Internationales Design Zentrum, Berlin (p 95); SONY
WALKMAN Sony (UK) Limited, Middlesex (p 100); THE TIZIO LAMP
The Design Museum (p 106); TUPPERWARE The Tupperware Company,
London (p 109); VESPA The National Motor Museum, Bealieu (p 113);
VOLKSWAGEN BEETLE N. Wright/The National Motor Museum,
Beaulieu (p 116); THE WASSILY CHAIR The Victoria and Albert Museum
(p 119); WOOLMARK International Wool Secretariat (p 11, p 120, p 121);
WORKMATE Black and Decker UK, Windsor and Christopher Forster,
Tekron International, Jersey for historical information on the Workmate
(p 123); Graham Ward; Jane Nolan and Enzostefano Manola of the
Design Museum; and with special thanks to Pat and David Steel for the
Lucky Strikes (p 67).

CONTENTS

INTRODUCTION

The term 'design' is currently in danger of losing any real meaning, debased as it is by such only partly-satirical manifestations as 'designer water', 'designer stubble' and the more cynical marketing ploys of 'designer jeans'. Much of this recent design consciousness has been superficial, and, in a predictable pattern repeated from the past — when such movements as art nouveau, art deco and Scandinavian modern suffered from commercial debasement — has masked what is, in essence, non-design. Despite this we have inherited from a century of design (or longer if we take the 1851 Great Exhibition as the starting point) irrevocable standards of function and construction which have benefitted the consumer.

Once attention shifts to aesthetics, however, a complex array of social, political and ethical forces come into play. For example, deplorable though the excesses produced by the American economic philosophy of planned obsolescence are considered to have been, it is arguable that design history would have been poorer had it not existed. On the other hand, planned obsolescence was shown to be not only an economic fallacy but socially damaging, and even whilst it was practised it was condemned by many as immoral.

To what extent then is moral responsibility essential to good design? Rather than hark back to the omnipresent Bauhaus, a contemporary example can be considered. Dieter Rams, who launched Braun onto its path of functionalist minimalism in 1955 (about the time when Virgil Exner and Harley Earl were gearing up to produce the ultimate in automobile kitsch), takes a broad overview: 'visual pollution is as powerful as physical pollution. Look at our cities — Tokyo, Los Angeles, Mexico City, even Frankfurt — they are all a mess of our creating. So when we design something new, why add to all the clutter? We need, if you like, as little design as possible.'

This seems plausible, even commendable, but nevertheless refuses to recognize that, just as T. S. Eliot stated that 'humankind cannot bear very

much reality', it may also have a limited capacity for design puritanism. Rams rationalizes Braun's mainly-matt-black philosophy (it used to be mainly white) by explaining that 'Braun products are serious products. Colour added for the sake of it would mean that they were less serious.' But clearly they are *not* 'serious' in the sense that, say, a brain scanner or a machine pistol could be so described. They are domestic consumer products, and by 'serious' Rams is presumably referring to the way they are designed and constructed, and perhaps implying that the consumer takes them seriously. In effect, matt black is itself 'entertaining' in that it enhances the aesthetic appeal of the objects.

This entertainment factor is inseparable from the totality of consumer design. Milner Gray gave an anecdotal explanation: 'It has been said that the perfectly functioning tea-pot – convenient to hold, pouring without spilling, and above all easy to clean – will inevitably be aesthetically satisfying. But something has been left out: the idea of visual enjoyment, of aesthetic pleasure. And if these are banished from the process of eating and drinking, nothing is left but the intake of carbohydrates and proteins.' Not only is Braun's matt black, in effect, decorative, it is also an important marketing ploy, a house style which is transmitting a coded message to the purchaser, saying (and only slightly more subtly than Coca-Cola) that this is the real thing.

Naturally, other manufacturers cashed in on this code, which led to a matt-black cult (heralded as a new phenomenon as though Wedgwood's 18th century black basalt ware never existed) which now seems to have played itself out. Already a reaction has set in, with 'high touch' poised to topple 'high tech' as a popularist design creed, whilst on the large stage, a battle rages between the champions of modern architecture and the neoclassicists.

Design is sometimes regarded as a disembodied art, yet historically it has always been indivisible from marketing. Obviously, there are areas where design and marketing are identical, as in packaging. There are also

instances where marketing colours our perceptions of the design, so, for example, it is unlikely that the *Zippo* lighter would have survived, attracting generation after generation of *aficionados*, had not its practical qualities been backed by the manufacturer's extraordinary guarantee of free repair. Conversely, had Rietveld's blue-and-red chair reached a mass market (in its original natural wood form) it would not have been artificially deified into an art object.

The bond between design and the market place had been articulated by a number of commentators by the mid 19th century: 'there are many influences outside the work itself which are important factors contributing to its design – for example, location, climate, time, custom, particular characteristics, rank, the position of the person for whom the work is intended and so on . . .' (Gottfried Sempter, *Science, Industry and Art*, 1852). The link was further expounded in the programme for the Deutscher Werkbund (1910), which stated that the association 'works for a cultural goal far beyond immediate specialized interests, with production work itself the main beneficiary. The association seeks its collaborators first of all in that area where production work proves accessible to refinement through artistic ideas. In pursuit of these effects it focuses its attention on the entire field of industry producing finished goods.' Prophetically, in 1915, Walter Gropius had written, 'As long as things are going well for the industrialist or the craftsman, that is, as long as he finds a market for his goods, no matter what sort or quality they may be, he will not consult the artist. But when he does, when things are going badly for him, he seeks him as he would seek the devil to sell his soul, determined to do anything to fill his threatened purse.' Gropius's cynical assessment is borne out by the evidence that some of the most intense moments in design history have occurred when industry was hard pressed to sell its products – Germany in the twenties, Britain and Italy immediately after the war, Japan in the late fifties and early sixties and the USA during the Depression.

Once it had seen the light, American industry embraced design with the fervour of the newly converted, to the extent that the 1939 New York World's Fair and, to a lesser degree, the 1933 Century of Progress in Chicago were design exhibitions. Henry Ford, who was as dismissive of art as he was of history, had been obliged to drop his 'any colour so long as it's black' axiom in response to the competition introducing colour to attract customers, and to bring out the 'designer' *Model A* in 1927. This belated recognition of design has been described as 'the most expensive art lesson in history'. Without this pressure Ford would, no doubt, have been content for the masses to be driving *Model T*s indefinitely. Although there was no established industrial design profession, one emerged, it seemed, almost overnight, its members drawn from architecture, engineering, graphic design and advertising. The father of American industrial design, Norman Bel Geddes, a graphic artist and theatre designer, opened the nation's first industrial design office in 1927. Within five years he had produced a range of ambitious design projects, including the 'flying wing' *Air Liner No. 4*, streamlined ships, cars and trains, as well as writing the first major book on industrial design, *Horizons* (1932), in which he defined the designer's role and methods. Geddes listed an analysis of the design objective — the intended function of a product, the way it is made, sold and serviced — as well as the manufacturer's capacity. Competitors' products would be examined, and extensive market research would be carried out. Not only would product costs be determined, but also the costs incurred in manufacturing, distribution and promotion. The same year as *Horizons* also saw the publication of Roy Sheldon and Egmont Arens's book *Consumer Engineering: A New Technique for Prosperity*, which blamed the poor economy on the moribund state of planning and marketing.

In 1929 the British manufacturer, Sigmund Gestetner, commissioned Raymond Loewy, already a well-established commercial artist who had been soliciting clients with the slogan, 'Between two products equal in

price, function and quality, the better looking one will outsell the other', to redesign the copying machine he produced. This project transformed the *Gestetner* from something that looked like a cross between an Edison cylinder phonograph and a 19th-century sewing machine into a compact device. This success, proved through increased sales, not only established Loewy's reputation (for his genius for self-promotion ensured that the *Gestetner* was fully exploited), but also encouraged other manufacturers to use industrial designers, as, for example, Kodak, for whom Walter Darwin Teague produced the stunning *Model 1A*. Within only a few years of the birth of American industrial design, not only consumer goods but major items – cars, ships and locomotives – were transformed, as statistics began to prove the increased sales that design stimulated. *Fortune* magazine, which had initially derided Geddes as a 'bomb thrower' whose radical concepts would cost American industry a billion dollars in retooling, had to recognize the commercial benefits which Loewy in particular constantly gave as the designer's *raison d'être*: 'industrial design keeps the customer happy, his client in the black and the designer busy' – or, as expressed on another occasion, the idea of the perfect line 'consists of a beautiful sales curve shooting upwards'.

By proving their credentials in the market place, designers gained credibility which in turn allowed them a degree of autonomy. Not only were their designs shaping their age, from mighty locomotives down to office staplers (but not the oft-cited Loewy streamlined pencil-sharpener, which never left the drawing board), providing a sense of identity and confidence which was celebrated in machine age art, but they were also working towards the future, as evidenced in the contributions of Geddes, Dreyfuss, Teague and Loewy to the World's Fair.

By its very nature, much design is necessarily ephemeral. Only rarely can it be judged as absolute, for its value is related to its historical context. For example, it is obvious that Geddes's airliner was based on the false assumption that transatlantic flight would be slow and that travellers

would therefore require the same facilities provided by an ocean liner, a design premise which was to be invalidated by jet engines. Similarly, the attempts by Téléavia, Phonola and Philco in the 1950s to reduce the bulk of the television set were made redundant by the subsequent arrival of electronic miniaturization and the slimline television tube. Not only are developments in technology sometimes unpredictable, they can also give rise to inconsistencies, such as the current revival of interest in traditional valve amplifiers, particularly amongst Japanese audiophiles, which has not only created a market for old equipment but also sufficient demand to warrant new state-of-the-art valve amplifiers going into production, despite the previous assumption that transistors had rendered the valve obsolete. This is not an exercise in nostalgia but a consequence of the fact that the quality of valve amplifiers is deemed to be superior.

A return to the past can also be seen in the re-introduction of both Peter Müller-Munk's 1948 *Waring* blender and the 1953 *Osterizer*, as well as other examples which refute Loewy's motto, 'Never Leave Well Enough Alone'. There is nothing stultifying in the effect of the past on current design. Not only does the longevity of such designs endorse them with the judgement of history, but by outliving their period they draw together the past and present to make design a living continuum. Some of these designs, now half a century old, seem destined for immortality.

By the simple test of survival, such designs warrant the accolade of 'classic', although this word has now become loosely used as a marketing term, as in the spurious 'modern classic' applied to something having no classic properties. To quote Milner Gray again: 'there is most certainly no universal formula by which good design can be either produced or assessed. It *can* be recognized, but we recognize it subjectively. We can pronounce *our* judgements; we cannot predict the future's . . .' The criterion by which the past is judged also lacks a 'universal formula', and its absence allows sufficient latitude for subjectively labelling a variety of disparate designs as 'classics' ∎

CERTIFICATION TRADE MARK
PURE NEW WOOL

THE AGA STOVE

Douglas Scott (Loewy Studios London) 1938

Until the consumer boom of the 1950s brought to kitchen appliances the reduced quality of construction and often spurious parade of new features that resulted from planned obsolescence, the cooker had been a solid device whose styling and marketing reflected the traditional lowly status of the kitchen. Although the concept of glamour was still alien to the kitchen, the influence of the late 19th and early 20th century awareness of hygiene had made ease of cleaning a major design criterion. It was this feature (as well as its versatility in also serving as a water heater and being independent of electricity or gas supplies) which originally made the *Aga* cooker popular.

The *Aga* stove also serves as an example of the designer's role in rationalizing and styling a well-proven object. Originally designed in Sweden (*Aga* being a merciful abbreviation of Svenska Akyiebolaget Gasacumulator), the cooker already existed as an efficient unit whose essential lines and characteristic heavily-enamelled surface were retained when it was restyled by Loewy's London studio in 1938. It is ironic that the *Aga*, which was originally a steadfastly modern design, has now joined its predecessor, the wood-burning stove, as an essential feature in the stripped pine surroundings of the 'traditional country kitchen'. Thus both nostalgically traditional and topically stylish at once — and with the bonus of fuel efficiency — its continuing popularity seems assured ■

Whilst other domestic cooking appliances have undergone numerous styling and technical changes, the stolid, almost puritanically gimmick-free *Aga* has endured — at home now in the most fashionable kitchen.

THE AIRSTREAM

Wally Byam 1934

Although the *Airstream* trailer and, above all, the promotion of it as a social liberator became Wally Byam's life's work, he only became involved in trailers by chance. Whilst proprietor of a do-it-yourself magazine he found himself under fire from readers complaining that the plans for a trailer featured in one issue were impractical. Working from these plans himself, he discovered the readers to be right, but at the same time he became fascinated by the project and set about his own design. His main discovery during this trial and error stage was that, by dropping the floor between the axles and making the roof higher, headroom for the user to stand upright was achieved. This in itself removed the stigma of cramped discomfort which had hitherto characterized trailers, an image which the *Airstream* later went on to repudiate as more and more amenities (water pumps, chemical toilets, kitchen facilities) were incorporated. Byam published a mail-order booklet of his own do-it-yourself plans for a trailer which could be built for less than $100, but also began making his own as a commercial venture. In 1930 he gave up other interests to become a full-time trailer builder.

Although its forerunner, the *Road Yacht* of 1928, was not particularly auspicious, being described as a 'large metal bug on wheels', when in 1934 he introduced the first *Airstream*, named to capitalize on the success of the Chrysler *Airflow*, it became a classic. Abandoning such traditional materials as plywood and composition board, he adopted the techniques of aircraft construction using riveted aluminium sheet and, in accordance with the styling craze which characterized much design of the period, streamlined contours. Although not aerodynamic in any scientific way, the *Airstream*'s lines nevertheless made the trailer easier to tow, whilst the all-aluminium construction gave it a greater strength-to-weight ratio than conventional frames.

Not only has the *Airstream* proved a durable commercial success – it is still in production – but it has become a cult – a fact which owes much to Wally Byam's paternalistic showmanship. To promote a fraternity of *Airstream* owners, as well as the products themselves, Byam organized *Airstream* treks to Europe and Africa, although he never achieved his ambition of seeing one of the Great Pyramids encircled by *Airstreams*. So important was this social aspect of American ownership that following his death in 1962 a foundation was set up to continue Byam's work ■

Like the
pioneer's
prairie wagon,
the *Airstream*
trailer still
stands for
freedom and
adventure.

THE ALADDIN LUNCHBOX

Aladdin Industries
1921

The *Aladdin* lunchbox has appeared in two guises – both as the original, classic domed-top tin workman's lunch box, which was introduced in 1921, and again, from 1957, with gaudy pop art decorations, as the school kit. Finished in functional black, the workman's box was equipped with two plated snap fasteners, and embossed ribbing gave the tin structure rigidity. The domed lid was designed to accommodate a thermos flask which the company also manufactured. By 1949 the box division of Aladdin was desperate to devise a way of increasing sales and, according to folklore, on impulse decided to embellish the plain-coloured school box with a picture of Hopalong Cassidy. Designed by Robert O. Burton, the *Hopalong* lunchbox instigated the pop lunchbox cult, with initial sales of fifty thousand, a figure which was soon eclipsed by Aladdin's rivals, KST, with the 1953 *Roy Rogers* lunchbox, which sold 2½ million in its first year. The traditional workman's dometop mutated into a school kit in 1957 with Burton's *Buccaneer*, since when it has appeared as a covered wagon for American Thermos's *Roy Rogers Chow Wagon* of 1958 and as a school bus in the all-time best seller, Aladdin's 1961 *Disney School Bus*. Seen either as a folk object from America's machine age of the twenties, or as a pop object of the fifties and sixties, the robust little lunchbox deserves our recognition ■

The black *Aladdin* lunchbox and thermos flask used to be the blue collar worker's badge of office until reincarnated (variously decorated) as a school kit.

THE ANGLEPOISE

George Cowardine
1934

Before its somewhat archaic and gawky appearance brought the *Anglepoise* lamp a new status as a retro design object, it had spent years as a severely practical device whose anonymity of style made it equally at home in an engineering shop or doctor's surgery. For most of its life it came in the same colour range as early Ford cars – black. This unself-conscious purity is typical of designs which have achieved a specific functional goal without any concessions to fashion or style. Although minor changes had occurred since its introduction in 1934, the *Anglepoise* remained essentially the same until 1978, when misguided attempts to modernize it only served to demonstrate the quality of the original.

The *Anglepoise* was initially designed by George Cowardine for his own use as a medical inspection lamp, the inspiration apparently being the articulation of the human arm.

To ensure that the lamp remained in whatever position it was adjusted to, springs were used as tension links. So crucial were the springs that the spring manufacturer, Herbert Terry and Sons (whose spring products included door closers), became the lamp's manufacturer.

The robust functionalism of the *Anglepoise* has not yet been bettered, for although the *Tizio* eclipsed it through sophistication, the practical bonuses of simplicity (it uses an ordinary household lamp bulb) and versatility (there are versions which clamp as well as wall-mounted ones) give it a range of application which ensures its continued usage ■

The timeless *Anglepoise* lamp was so commonplace that its gawky, archaic look was taken for granted until attempts to modernize it served to reveal its robust practicality.

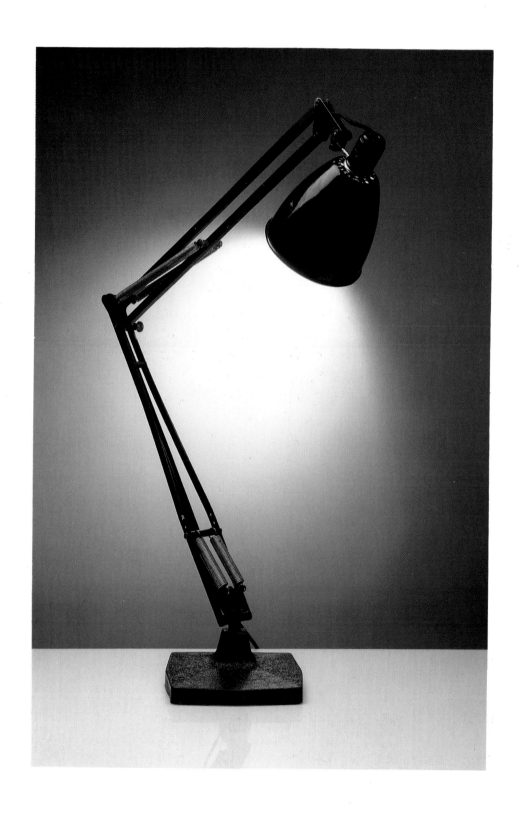

Despite Tom Wolfe's satirical denigration, the *Barcelona* chair remains a cult design object, a status which sometimes detracts from its true qualities. (Picture courtesy of Knoll International)

THE BARCELONA CHAIR

Ludwig Mies van der Rohe 1929

Representing as it does the epitome of non-egalitarian Bauhaus design, and being designed by another pet hate, Ludwig Mies van der Rohe (whom he referred to as White God No. 2), Tom Wolfe had a field day satirizing the cult status of the *Barcelona* chair in *From Bauhaus to Our House*. In it, he relates how, in the late forties, owning the *Barcelona* chair was *de rigueur* for every young American architect: 'When you saw that holy object on the sisal rug, you knew you were in a household where a fledgling architect and his young wife had sacrificed everything to bring the symbol of the godly mission into their home. Five hundred and fifty dollars! She had even given up the diaper service and was doing the diapers by hand. It got to the point where, if I saw a *Barcelona* chair, no matter where, I immediately – in the classic stimulus-response bond – smelled diapers gone high.'

The *Barcelona* chair had never been intended to be other than an expensive piece of furniture, and unlike for example Marcel Breuer's tubular steel *Wassily* armchair, or the various cantilever chairs designed by Breuer, Mart Stam and Mies van der Rohe, it was not intended for mass production nor a mass market, as evidenced by its expensive strip steel and leather construction. It was, in fact, custom designed for the German pavilion at the 1929 World's Fair in Barcelona, and represented the ideal of an integration between architecture and the building's furnishing that had been prefigured in the 1927 Weissenhof housing project, for which he designed the *Weissenhof* tubular steel armchair (which featured a canework seat by Lilly Reich), and which would be further exemplified in 1930 by chairs designed for the Tugendhat house. The *Barcelona* chairs, with their complementary footstools, reflected the luxury of the pavilion itself, which featured a pool surround of green marble and a free-standing onyx wall. With such a background, it is not surprising that the chair, still in production, has remained synonymous with luxurious style ■

BEL GEDDES: AIR LINER NO. 4

Although the realization of a design in a tangible form

Norman Bel Geddes
with Dr Otto Koller
1929

satisfies the test of fulfilment, and although there are many subsequent tests — of which consumer acceptance and market endurance are the most obvious — a case can nevertheless be made for conceptual designs, which though existing in a timeless vacuum have their own reality. The incongruous juxtaposition of the designs of Leonardo da Vinci and Heath Robinson can be cited as examples of concepts where the question as to whether they would work in practice is almost superfluous. The automobile industry is constantly engaged in technical and styling research, only a small proportion of which will actually be put into practice; and, in like manner, Raymond Loewy's 1933 streamlined pencil-sharpener is so credible as a design that it has acquired its own reality, being commonly referred to as though it actually existed as a production item. Norman Bel Geddes was not only a pioneer industrial designer but also looked beyond professional work for clients to theoretical and self-initiated design projects. Although *Air Liner No. 4* never went into production, it was no academic exercise, but a real and thorough examination of the logistics of transatlantic air travel in the late twenties.

Geddes's ambition was initially a plane which, as he later described it in *Horizons*, would get 'a thousand luxury-lovers from New York to Paris fast. Forget the limitations.' The *Air Liner* serves as an extreme example of how a design cannot do more than aspire to maximize the technology available at the time, for it was designed quite literally as the aviation equivalent of a luxury ship. Geddes was working on the assumption that at an average cruising speed of 100 m.p.h., the Chicago–London route would take 42 hours, and the plane would therefore have to offer the same accommodation and recreation facilities that a liner would. Staterooms and suites would have bathrooms, complete with running water; there was to be a promenade deck, a lounge, dining rooms and restaurants, a barber's shop and a beauty salon, a gymnasium, a nursery, a library and a sickbay. There was to be a high ratio of crew to passengers (the plane's maximum would have been 451 travellers) with 115 crew members, including hairdressers, masseurs, a librarian, nursemaids, a doctor and nurses and even a wine steward.

Every detail of the *Air Liner* was fully worked out. Its concept of luxury transatlantic air travel was not so fanciful, for it was offering little more in terms of facilities than the commercial *Zeppelins* had. Furthermore, there already existed another role model, Claude Dornier's 1929 *DO-X* flying boat. The flying boat was literally that – the use of water for landing and take off providing the answer to the problem of stress which would otherwise have affected its 48 tons. The body of the *DO-X* was more boat than plane, and even included porthole windows. The Dornier, the world's biggest aircraft at the time, could carry 150 passengers.

If nothing else, *Air Liner No. 4* exemplifies the utter confidence with which designers of the time viewed the machine age. The engineering of the *Air Liner* was entrusted to Dr Otto Koller, who had been the German military's chief aeronautical engineer and who had designed over 200

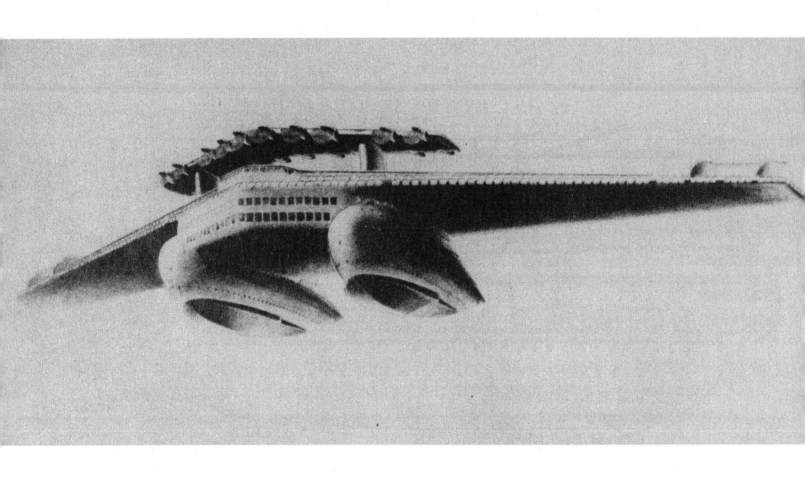

Destined to
remain forever
a design
exercise, *Air
Liner No. 4*
epitomizes the
concept of
luxurious, if
leisurely,
transatlantic
flying.

planes. The *Air Liner* was in essence a tail-less 528-foot flying wing which was to sit on two enormous streamlined floats. The plane was equipped with twenty engines, with a further six for back up in the event of engine failure. It was to carry not only six lifeboats but also two small planes which could be launched from it whilst in flight!

Despite its image as a Buck Rogers space vehicle, Geddes originally intended that *Air Liner No. 4* should be in production by 1940. How it would have fared in practice will never be known, though the design is considered to be technically sound. Frozen forever in the design stage though it was, it nevertheless represents an historical achievement; the flying wing concept has remained on the outer edges of aeronautical engineering.

The inventor of the flying wing, John Knudson Northrup, had been a founder of the Lockheed Aircraft Company, and had produced his first flying wing in 1928, undoubtedly inspiring Geddes's *Air Liner*. The advantages of the flying wing were its high capacity-to-weight ratio and its inherent structural strength. Northrup's design was adopted by the US Navy as an ideal long-range bomber. Although the huge *XB-35* (which weighed 165,000 lbs and could carry a crew of fifteen) was built it did not fly until 1946. In 1947 jet engines replaced the under-powered propeller engines, but the very technology that had finally made it viable proved its downfall when it was deemed that the future lay in conventionally shaped jet aeroplanes ■

THE BERTOIA CHAIR

Harry Bertoia 1952

Harry Bertoia had initially worked as a silver-smith, and the famous *Bertoia* chair evolved from his experimental wire structures. Although his *Diamond* chair (1952) for Knoll International and subsequent chairs were originally designed to be covered in a moulded foam-backed fabric the chairs are normally seen uncovered, their structure evidence of Bertoia's claim that the chairs were objects in space, that 'space passes right through them'. Bertoia has stated that 'the urge for good design is the same as the urge to go on living. The assumption is that somewhere, hidden, is a better way of doing things.' His approach to design is essentially practical, as is demonstrated by his use of bonded rubber mounts to link the lightweight seat shell to the welded steel rod base-frame. This allows for a flexibility between the base and the seat, introducing a resilience to the chair which would otherwise have been rigid owing to the tensile strength of the seat's mesh construction. *Bertoia* chairs and footstool have remained one of Knoll International's most enduring designs ■

The concept of the chair as sculptural statement did not lessen the functional correctness of Bertoia's 'objects in space'.

THE BRAUN SK SERIES RADIOGRAMOPHONES

Dieter Rams and
Hans Gugelot 1956

Braun's *SK* radiogramophone has several claims to being a landmark in domestic audio equipment, the most obvious being its innovative introduction of the transparent lid, a feature which has become a standard design element ever since.

Max Braun had pioneered the radiogramophone with an integral record player and radio (as opposed to the two elements being incorporated separately in a cabinet) with the *Phono Super 6740W* in the late thirties, but only very few went into production, and ironically neither Dieter Rams nor Hans Gugelot were aware of this historical background when they designed the *SK4* in 1956.

Although the *SK4* appeared almost clinical in comparison with its contemporaries, it nevertheless represented a continuation of Hans Gugelot's concept of 'sound furniture' which had developed through earlier radio sets. Aesthetically, this 'sound furniture' was the antithesis of what Gugelot's biographer, Herbert Lindinger, described as 'the bourgeois preference to hide technical devices in living room furniture', and Braun's first Head of Design, Dr Fritz Eichler, credited the *SK4* with probably doing 'more to distinguish Braun design than any other product'.

Whilst not a feature of the original design, the transparent lid of 'Snow White's Coffin' (as in the *SK61* illustrated) introduced a feature which was to become standard for virtually all record players.

Although Braun's design puritanism sometimes seems somewhat self-conscious, the *SK*'s transparent acrylic lid introduced a rare — although unintended — element of humour, quickly earning the otherwise impeccable unit the nicknames of 'Snow White's coffin' and 'die beautifully'. Even though the transparent top was to be universally adopted as a standard element for record players, it nevertheless represented a compromise of Gugelot's original concept.

The *SK* was designed as a fundamentally new approach to cabinet construction, which had invariably been of wood, either in the form of a simple box, or of the various 'bourgeois' furniture pastiches. Gugelot's radical solution was to take Dieter Rams's layout and house it in a U-shaped metal case with wooden endpieces. The original intention was to have a metal lid, following the lines of the main cabinet. Both aesthetically (Dieter Rams has been quoted as saying that it looked like a bread box) and technically (the metal created resonance and tended to rattle) the metal lid was unsatisfactory. For the initial publicity, the first few introduced were photographed with the lid taken off. Logically, the transparent top, which had the bonus of putting the record deck, radio tuning dial and controls knobs — all of which demonstrated an unpreced-

ented attention to style and meticulous order – on show, was the nearest approximation to having no top. The attention to detail which characterized the layout was echoed in every aspect, with everything from buttons to lid hinges being specially designed.

The *SK4* was immediately lauded as a design achievement, gaining a prize at the 1957 Milan Triennale and a place in the Museum of Modern Art in New York's permanent collection in 1958. Unlike some designs which are thus honoured but never transcend a rather sterile, precious status as 'design objects', the *SK* was commercially successful, continuing in production with a series of technical changes until 1963.

THE CITROEN 2CV

Pierre Boulanger
1939

The *2CV* only appears eccentric when judged by current standards of pseudo-sophistication; it epitomized the application of lateral design thinking and innovative engineering to the utility motor car.

Although the *2CV* did not survive the eighties, its longevity has ensured its position, together with the Volkswagen *Beetle*, as an improbable motoring classic. According to folklore, the design brief was to produce an economy car, a new *Motel T* Ford, in which a peasant could carry a basket of eggs across a field without any breakages. This was achieved by means of an innovative self-levelling suspension, with horizontal coil springs linking the front and rear sections. To further counteract an uneven ride, seating was designed with canvas over simple tubular steel frames producing a gimbal-like effect. When the project began in 1936, Citroen's chief designer, Pierre Boulanger, described the goal as 'an umbrella on four wheels'.

Although not the smallest car on the market (it was longer than the Fiat *500*, Austin *A30* and *4CV* Renault) it only measured 3.75 metres in length, yet achieved a high ratio of usable space for its size. The strictly utilitarian nature of the vehicle dictated a very simple body shell, with easily removable doors and a hood with interlocking flanges instead of hinges. The roof area was almost entirely taken up by a canvas panel which could be rolled back, and, in strict accordance with its concept of minimalism, the original design had only one headlamp and one windscreen wiper.

Despite the very basic structure of the *2CV*, it was by no means primitive technically. Without compromising the requirements of simple construction and maintenance which had dictated the body design, the car featured sophisticated engineering, not only in its suspension but also in the front wheel drive via an air-cooled flat twin engine and a synchromesh four-speed gearbox. With a top speed of some 40 m.p.h., fuel consumption was an economical 57 miles per gallon.

By 1939 250 *2CV*s had been produced, all save one being destroyed to stop them falling into enemy hands. The survivor was dismantled and hidden. This little cell proved to be the saviour of the French automobile industry, for the *2CV* was back in production in 1948. In 1953 manufacture also started in Britain, where its customers included the Navy, who used it in its pick-up form as a dockside stores delivery vehicle, as well as a potentially useful helicopter-carried jeep. Although through its history much of its spartan quality was lost in a series of improvements (the single headlamp, single windscreen wiper frugality only applied to the early ones), the *2CV* retained an undeniable individualism which has made it one of the last eccentric, 'personality' cars ■

COCA-COLA

Chapman Root Glass
Co, Indiana USA 1915

Coca-Cola were pioneers of marketing and, from their early days, intuitively established a corporate identity. Although Raymond Loewy often cited Coca-Cola as clients, and although he did in fact design such items as bottle chests, syrup dispensers and a delivery truck in the forties, there is doubt (cast by no lesser people than Coca-Cola themselves) over his claims that he had any hand in the ultimate, universal symbol, the *Coca-Cola* bottle, surely the most successful packaging of all time.

So recognizable is the *Coca-Cola* bottle (Coca-Cola claim it is known to 90% of the world's population) that on several occasions during the company's history it has been used in isolation as an advertising motif, without any extraneous information, and in 1960 the bottle itself was registered as a trademark. In fact, the famous bottle was not originated by the Coca-Cola Company, whose products during the early years would appear in a variety of conventionally straight-sided bottles which were supplied by the individual bottling plants. The famous 'hobble skirt', or, as it is sometimes known, *Mae West* bottle was introduced by the Chapman Root Glass Company of Indiana in 1915. Its qualities have been detailed by Raymond Loewy in a letter to Coca-Cola, where he described it as 'a masterpiece of scientific functional planning', listing its features as being able to be held easily by any size of hand, even when wet, being impact resistant due to the thickness of the glass and the fact that 'the so-called locked-stresses within the glass structure tend to resist implosive as well as explosive damage in spite of violent percussive action upon the impact point'. The classic bottle design was first patented on 16 November 1915 and again on 25 December 1923 (it is also known as the *Thanksgiving* or *Christmas* bottle) as well as on various subsequent occasions, an indication of how seriously Coca-Cola regarded it as a marketing tool. With over two thousand cities bottling *Coca-Cola*, the unifying effect of a common bottle was an important factor in product identification, and the 'hobble skirt' became immediately featured in advertising campaigns, including such promotional items as *Coca-Cola* whistles. In the 1920s there were promotional lamps in the form of the bottle, and in the 1930s a bottle-shaped radio, as well as countless advertising premiums celebrating the already-famous icon of soft drink. The *Coca-Cola* bottle's finest hour was undoubtedly during World War II, when the company pledged that America's fighting forces would be supplied with *Coca-Cola* wherever they were in action, establishing overseas bottling plants to do so.

Iconized by Pop Artists and centrepiece of countless advertise-ments, the *Coca-Cola* bottle has taken on a symbolic role which surpasses its function as packaging.

In 1955 the bottle was subtly changed: it lost some of its bulbous, chunky contours and white paint replaced its heavy, raised lettering, which eventually became worn in the cleaning processes, sometimes acquiring an almost sand-blasted look. Even this simplified version has succumbed to a restyling which has finally severed all links with the *Coke* bottle tradition. Although this has not been seen as the same level of betrayal as the 1985 introduction of New *Coke* (which promoted some connoisseurs to lay down some Old *Coke* as they would fine wine – though it was quickly reprieved and is now known as Classic *Coke*), it nevertheless means that the visual and tactile (as well as practical, if Loewy was right) properties of the original bottle are now lost. For those to whom the thick, distinctive glass bottle was inherently part of *Coca-Cola*, the 'real thing' is no longer quite so real ■

THE COLDSPOT REFRIGERATOR

Raymond Loewy 1934

The 1934 *Coldspot Super Six* refrigerator has several claims to fame. It was the first to be marketed for its appearance as well as other features, thereby introducing the importance of *image* to domestic appliances – a factor which in the fifties would result in the doctrine of planned obsolescence bringing to the kitchen the same sort of constant restyling that Detroit went in for (including fashion colours and even two-tone refrigerators). It was also the first time that a mass-produced consumer item followed the direction pioneered by Gestetner, who, in commissioning Loewy to redesign their duplicating machine in 1929, had vindicated not only Loewy himself but also the very role of the industrial designer. For the *Coldspot*, Loewy not only completely re-designed the casework (as with the *Gestetner*, adopting the sculptural technique of evolving the form in clay, which was subsequently to become a standard practice in automobile design) but also rationalized the fittings, including the hinges and door handles, as well as introducing a new form of aluminium shelving. By rationalizing the refrigerator produc-tion costs were reduced, enabling Sears to advertise it as being half the price of other makes. In bringing the concept of design to the lower end of the market, the *Coldspot* pioneered the permeation of modernism through virtually every aspect of life which occurred during the thirties and which culminated in the 1939 World's Fair being, in effect, a design showcase ■

Before planned obsolescence debased domestic appliances, the *Coldspot* refrigerator was a model of the style and economy achievable through rational design.

CONCORD POWERFLOOD

Robert Heritage 1969

Concord Lighting emerged from Rotaflex in the 1960s to market the growing spotlight range which it had pioneered for commercial, industrial and domestic use. Having introduced an acknowledged classic fitting with the *Teardrop* light in 1956, Rotaflex had actively pursued the concept of designed lighting, teaming design consultants with their own technical staff, so that, for example, Terence Conran was provided with thirteen staff for the development of the *Targa* range. Robert Heritage's *Powerflood* of 1969 has become an enduring classic light fitting. Used for 'lightwashing' walls, and available either ceiling or track mounted, the *Powerflood* uses reflectors designed to cast an even light with a very definite cut-off at the top and bottom. The *Powerflood* utilizes the traditional theatre light's 'barn door' flaps to direct the light, but there is no sense of its being merely an updated version of the theatrical ancestor. The heat from the tungsten halogen bulbs (up to 500W) is not lost through the traditional louvres but is dispersed through the large surface area of the lamp's cast alloy body, achieved through the use of deep fins. Still in extensive use, the *Powerflood* has been recognized by numerous design awards.

The *Powerflood* combined scientific lighting design with a style evocative of theatre floods.

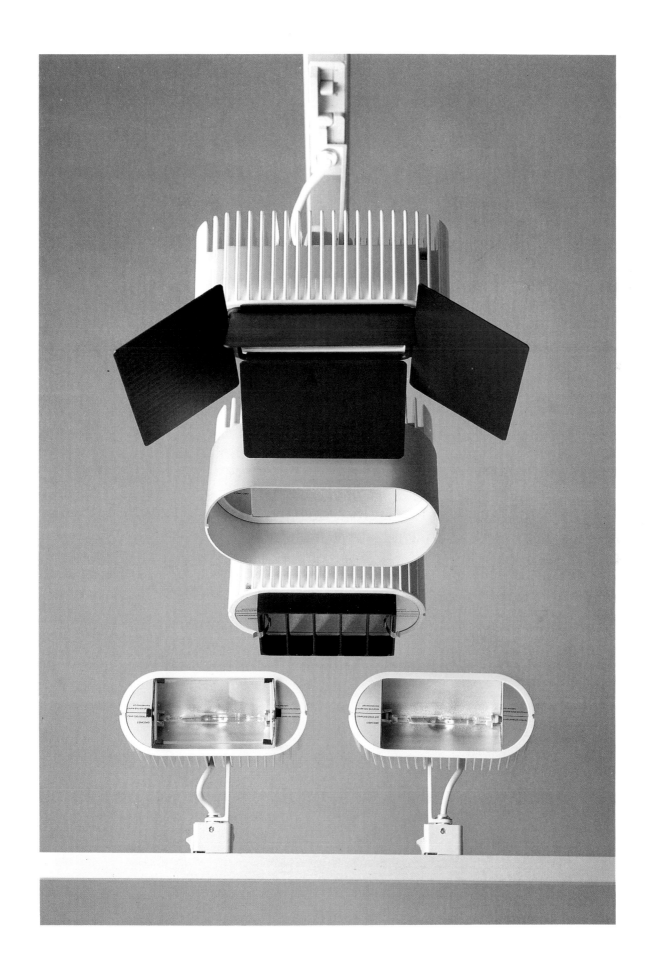

DESOUTTER ELECTRIC DRILLS

Desoutter Bros. c.1950

Desoutter is best known for being one of the world's major manufacturers of pneumatic tools, including sophisticated units for specialized industrial applications, but the company was also an early pioneer of electric power tools, which it began manufacturing in 1929. In 1979 the company dropped its electric range in favour of pneumatics, leaving behind a fifty-year legacy of innovation which, in effect, created the modern electric drill.

Its most important contribution was the reduction of both weight and bulk. Previously, a ¼″ chuck capacity drill (the smallest size) would have weighed at least 6lbs, often more, so that single-handed use was almost impossible. Desoutter redesigned the electric motor, so that its bulk was considerably reduced without any loss of power. The lower motor brush was incorporated with the switch in the pistol-style grip, thus balancing the weight distribution. The use of an ergonomically designed light, silicon-alloy casing, which was vented to ensure that, despite the lack of space around it, the motor was efficiently cooled, resulted in a total weight of just 2lbs, and the combination of lightweight construction and balance allowed single-handed operation. Subsequent developments in electric drills, such as the use of plastic casing and the cordless, battery-operated drill, have not succeeded in bettering the *Desoutter* in terms of compactness and lightness.

The unique Desoutter *corner drill (top), together with the compact ¼″ drill (below) achieved an unsurpassed power-to-size ratio.*

Although the drill throughout its production was housed in a rather Buck Rogers space-pistol style of casing, the company also produced a *Streamline* version whose smooth contours were achieved at the expense of easy access to the motor for repairs and servicing, with the result that rather than sacrifice practicality to aesthetics, the line was discontinued.

Whilst the small ¼″ capacity drill is the most familiar example of state-of-the-art power tool design (the company also produced heavier duty drills, as well as accessories and special purpose electric tools), it does not represent the ultimate in compactness. This was achieved by the Desoutter *A Series* (later re-designated *CD*) corner drills, where the drill was at right angles to the body of the tool instead of the conventional in-line arrangement. Whereas the closeness with which a normally constructed drill could be used in a restricted space was limited by the size

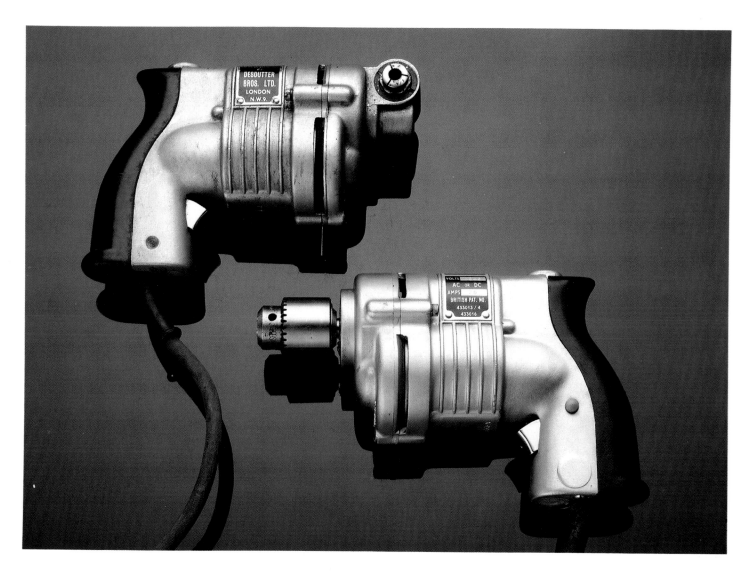

of the drill body, the *CD* could be used within ½″ of the facing surface of a right-angled area.

Technology can be a double-edged sword, for whilst the Desoutter drills exemplified high tech for many years, in the end technology brought about their demise. The safety requirements of double insulation (which, ironically, was first used on the American *Millers Falls* small electric drill of 1960, in which Garth Huxtable's design shows a strong Desoutter influence) could not be incorporated in the drills without drastic redesigning. Paradoxically, the price of progress in this case proved to be the loss of some of the most interesting electric tools ever made ■

THE EKCO AD 75

Wells Coates
1934–1946

Describing the history of British radio design in *Design 46*, the handbook of the 'Britain Can Make It' Exhibition, Professor R. D. Russell characterized the products of the period that linked the early radios (where the speaker was an external horn) and the designed sets of the thirties (some of which were the work of Russell himself) as 'a series of lamentable designs (at their best negatively undistinguished period hashes; at their worst modernistic jazz)', commenting that the only redeeming feature was that during this time the radio became established as a piece of home equipment and was no longer 'a laboratory gadget'.

Up to the late twenties, the design qualities had been irrelevant, for the public appeal of radio was in the medium itself. The transformation into an item of domestic furnishing only came about once it had ceased to be a diverting novelty. The General Strike of 1926 (when newspapers had been reduced to basic information sheets) demonstrated the value of the radio for news and entertainment. In 1927 the BBC was incorporated under the directorship of the legendary J. G. W. Reith, broadcasting nationally to over two million licencees. At this time, the crystal set was being superseded by the mains-powered valve radio, and the public, flocking to the annual radio exhibition Radiolympia, were eager to buy the products of the newly emerging industry.

E. C. Cole Ltd (Ekco), a major manufacturer, pioneered the use of moulded bakelite with their *Model 313* of 1930. The severe functionalism of the *313* was mellowed in its successor, the *SH25* (designed by J. K. White) which, in common with many other products, simply used bakelite as a literal substitute for wood. The appearance of the *SH25* was little different from a wood cabinet, even to the willow tree speaker-grille motif, itself reminiscent of the fretwork which was a common feature of the do-it-yourself cabinet designs of the contemporary hobbyists' magazines.

Having committed themselves to bakelite, Ekco took the dramatic step of commissioning the architect and designer Serge Chermayeff, whose *Model AC 64* of 1933 represented a total break with the homely, folksy look. For the next year's models, Ekco held a competition amongst leading architects and designers. Chermayeff was again chosen, and indeed his *Model 74*, which had a more pronounced moulded appearance, a prominent semi-circular tuning dial and large control knobs, achieved a genuine fusion of technology and style. As an exemplification of modernity, however, it was eclipsed by the other successful submission, again the work of an architect-designer, Wells Coates. The Ekco *AD 65* took an unprecedented circular form which served to focus attention on the speaker area, above which a semi-circular tuning dial, as with

The Ekco
Model AD 75
(pictured) was
one of several
various on
Wells Coates's
striking
circular design.

Chermayeff's design, emphasized the range which the radio could receive. Like the *Model 74*, Coates's design was available either in brown (although the unequivocally moulded form demonstrated that here brown bakelite was not being used as ersatz wood) or black. For the first time in radio design, the black version was enlivened with chrome, itself the badge of modernity and still an important part of present day design language. Whilst retaining its circular form, the *AD 65* was transmuted through successive models, making its last appearance in the 'Britain Can Make It' Exhibition as the *A22*, in which the case was reduced to a slender frame.

Although less obviously a design object, the *AD 75* has a closer link between its form and function and emanates a stronger 'radio' presence. Here, the tuning dial, reduced to a neat, semi-circular band, is repositioned beneath the speaker and directly above the knobs, consolidating the functions and emphasizing their purpose. To follow the line of the tuning band, the speaker grille loses its circular shape and appears as a crescent, relieved by slender, curved bands of bakelite.

The contribution of Ekco to radio design was relatively short-lived. World War II brought about a shortage both of radio receivers and essential valves, whilst post-war design saw a return to the extensive use of wood. The radio itself became eclipsed by television, losing the pride of place it had enjoyed as a domestic item in the thirties.

The circular Ekco radio, left behind by these and subsequent developments, remains an outstanding example of art deco styling, a monument to Ekco's patronage of modern design ■

THE ERICOFON

Ralph Lysell
Gosta Thomas
Hugo Blomberg
1956

The liberation of the telephone during the last decade has seen not only a proliferation of novelty instruments (the ultimate kitsch example of which, the Mickey Mouse phone, will no doubt gain historical significance as the embodiment of that liberation) but also the freedom created by doing away with the umbilical cord, in the case of car phones and cordless phones. The latter, with their combination of high tech and high public-nuisance value, have become the modern equivalent of the early transistor radios. Inevitably, the increasing variety has brought about the belated recognition of the inherent qualities of such instruments as Jean Heiberg's design – for many years the archetypal British telephone – or Henry Dreyfuss's Bell telephone, though this recognition is often alloyed with a strong element of retro chic.

The dominant presence of these two instruments gives the false

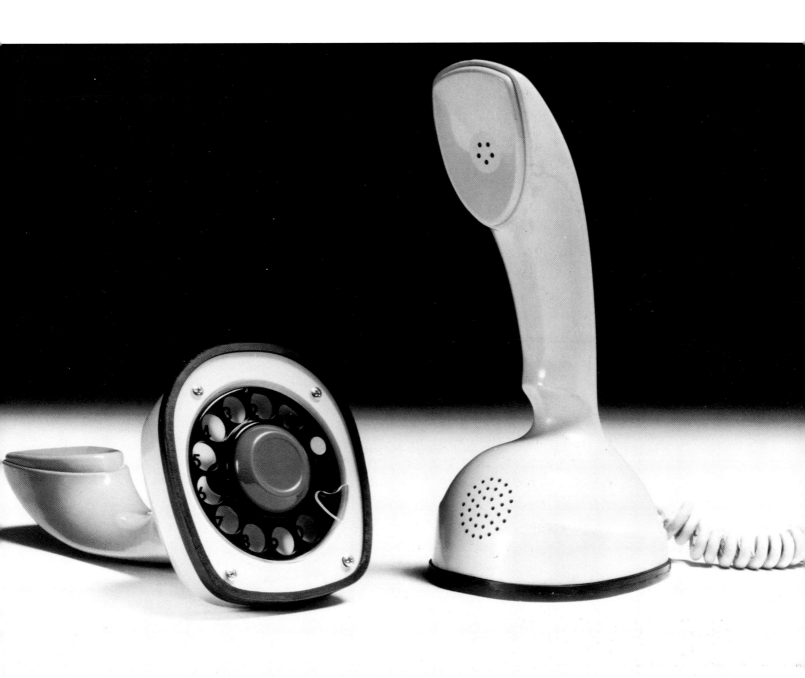

By incorporating the dial in the base, the *Ericofon* became the first integrated single unit telephone.

impression that innovative designs are a new phenomenon, so much so that the 1956 *Ericofon* is often assumed to be far more recent. Originally conceived by Ralph Lysell in 1941, and redesigned by Lysell, Gosta Thomas and Hugo Blomberg for production by L. M. Ericson, the instrument caused a sensation when first demonstrated to the independent telephone industry's convention in Chicago by the North Company of Ohio. Predating Dreyfuss's *Trimline* phone for Bell by nearly ten years, the *Ericofon* was the first instrument to break from the traditional two-piece format. With all functions incorporated in a single moulded case of lightweight styrene, it is built around the handset, the bottom half of which incorporates the dial and speaker. Although the *Ericofon* was as robustly built as more obviously solid telephones, it suffered from the fact that the telephone itself was still seen first and foremost as a commercial instrument, a piece of office equipment – a factor which was a major influence on the design of the *Trimline*. Because of this, the pioneering value of the *Ericofon* was not so much its technology, although its lightweight construction was important, but its presentation of the telephone as an attractive item. As home phones became more widespread, along with the use of one or more extensions, the domestic market became sufficiently important to justify such elements as colour and elegance as design criteria for telephones.

Although ahead of its time, the *Ericofon* is distinguished not only as a design solution but also as one of the instigators of the liberation of the telephone ■

THE FALCON PIPE

Kenley Bugg 1940

Whilst most pipes are made in an old established craft tradition, either conforming to conventional shapes or occasionally taking on some unusual form, there have also been a vast number of system pipes designed to overcome problems of overheating and hygiene. One of the most obviously 'designed' pipes is the *Porsche*, the work of Ferdinand Alexander Porsche, the car designer. Introduced in 1984, it uses the same engineering principle as aero-engine cylinders, cooling the pipe's bowl with a ribbed aluminium casing which increases the surface area in order to dissipate heat. The pipe's high-tech look evokes the advantageous marketing associations of the Porsche name.

Whilst devoid of the *Porsche*'s glamour, the *Falcon* pipe has the advantage of achieving an economical, if less stylish solution. Invented by an American engineer, Kenley Bugg, the *Falcon* first appeared in 1940. By making only the upper bowl of wood, which screws into a metal lower bowl and stem, problems of overheating and cleaning were overcome. This modular system also had the advantage that, by introducing new designs of bowl and stem whilst retaining their interchangeability, the consumer could play around with various permutations. Eventually 7

The *Falcon* pipe's unconventional two-part design made possible mass production as well as creating a vast range of possible styles.

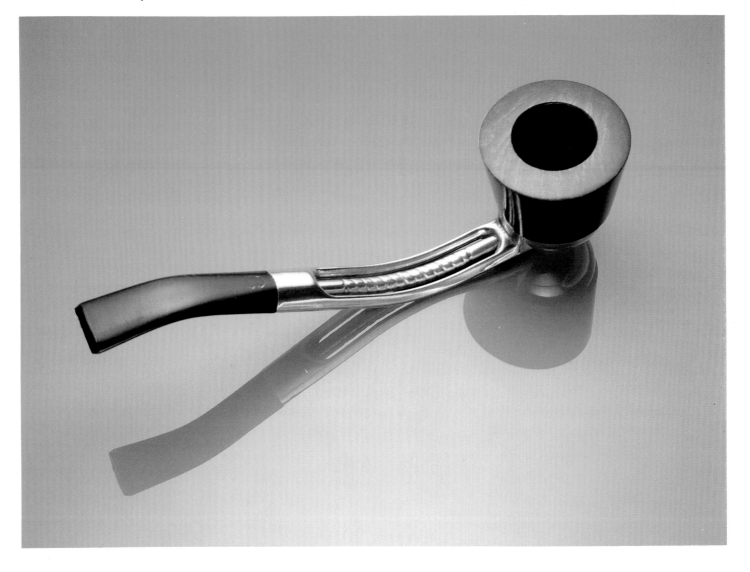

stem styles and 48 bowls led to a possible 13,680 different pipes from this system. The *Falcon* came into the market at a period when the public was particularly receptive to modernity in all things, and even though the pipe's futuristic appearance has undeniably dated and been diluted by the inclusion in the range of some traditional styles, over a million *Falcons*, now made in Britain, are still sold annually to a world-wide market ■

THE FENDER STRATOCASTER

Leo Fender and
Leo Tavares 1953

Although other electric guitars have incorporated more sophisticated technology and possess other qualities which distinguish them, the *Stratocaster* enjoys a special position as an enduring icon of rock music. As an instrument, the '*Strat*' produces a unique sound, whilst the visual impact of its characteristic shape has lost none of its power in 37 years, and is even now a model for various copies. Its asymmetric double-horned shape (its forerunner, the Fender *Broadcaster* – later renamed the *Telecaster* – of 1948 and the Gibson *ES5* both had a single horn) spurned any resemblance to the body contours of the traditional acoustic guitar, dramatizing the essential difference between them. This difference lies in the physical emission of sound from the strings, and is so fundamental that one school of thought holds the solid-bodied electric guitar to be a separate instrument in its own right.

The *Stratocaster* was introduced in 1953. Its designers – Leo Fender and Leo Tavares – had been, alongside Paul Bigsby and Les Paul, pioneers of the electric guitar in the forties. Although Les Paul's 'the Plank' (a prototype literally made from a railtrack sleeper in the late thirties) is credited with being the first solid-bodied electric guitar, Fender and Tavares's *Broadcaster* was the first to go into production. Along with its radical shape, whose slab-like appearance conceals a subtle contouring of the back which both reduces its weight and makes it easier to hold against the player's body, the *Stratocaster* was technically innovative, featuring for the first time in a commercially produced instrument three pick-ups and a vibrola arm which activates a pitch change, and which in the case of the Fender has the unique characteristic of always returning to its previous pitch with unerring accuracy.

As well as still being played, the *Stratocaster* also has the charisma of historic associations, its very appearance instantly evoking images of, for example, the legendary Jimi Hendrix ■

Quite apart from the quality of the sound it produces, the Fender *Stratocaster* possesses a charisma which has made it not just another guitar, but an icon of rock music.

THE HAMILTON BEACH DRINKMASTER

Hamilton Beach Co.
c.1930

Still in production, although restyled, the *Drinkmaster* is an enduring link with the America of the thirties. Its base and stem are vitreous-enamelled in the ubiquitous Depression green, and it comes with its folk memories of the diners of which it was a mandatory feature. Although other manufacturers, such as Gilchrist, produced similarly styled mixers, the Hamilton Beach *Model 30* best combines simple elegance and function, its switch-actuated paddle starting as soon as the stainless steel drink flask is put in place, enabling speedy service and allowing the machine to be devoid of any external controls. Although it is the single mixer which is the definitive model, there were also triple versions, and the same basic lines of the *Model 30* also appeared in the *No. 20 Arnold* malted milk dispenser — which measured out quantities of powder using a mechanism similar to a gumball machine — and an *en suite* heavy-duty orange press ■

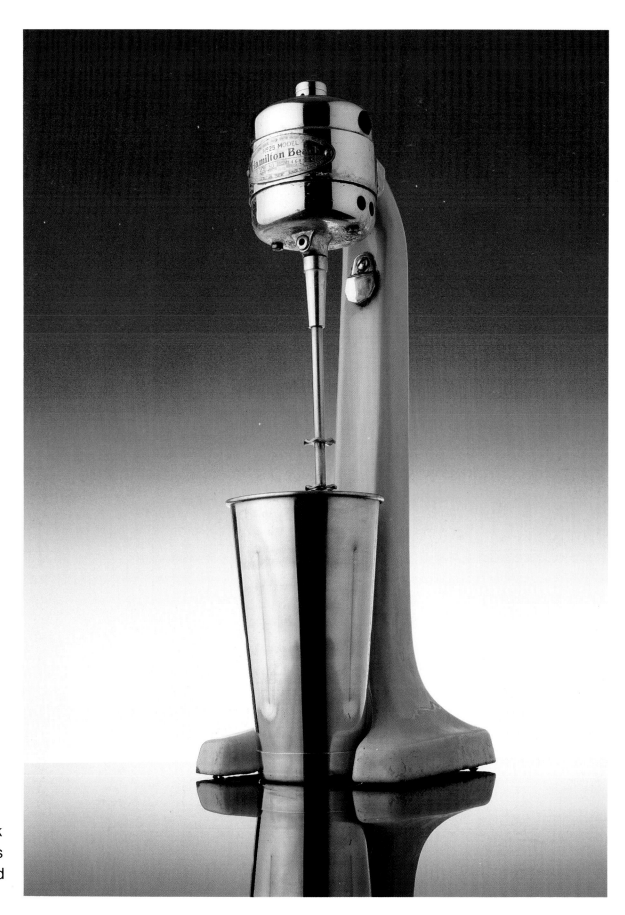

The original *Drinkmaster* evokes the traditional diners and milk bars where it is still to be found in use.

THE HMV ELECTRIC CONVECTOR HEATER

Christian Barman
1934

The majority of electric heaters are of the radiant type and have with varying degrees of success featured the reflector as the dominant design element. It is also fairly standard that the design seeks to disguise the true nature of the appliance as an ersatz coal or log fire, a practice which still continues. By contrast, Christian Barman's 1934 *HMV Electric Convector Heater* owes more to the influence of lighting design than other electric items and reveals the designer's architectural background. Indeed while working as a publicity officer for the London Passenger Transport Board between 1935 and 1941, alongside Frank Pick, he also contributed designs for bus shelters, platform seating and other fittings. The heater's stepped parabolic curves of either chromed or enamelled metal are entirely functional, both storing and directing the heat, yet the overall effect is of stunning styling. Though not streamlined in the strictest sense, the *HMV Heater* nevertheless displays the aesthetics of Streamline Modern and as such can be regarded as a classic embodiment of the spirit of that movement.

The smooth contours of Christian Barman's *HMV Heater* make it an untypically successful example of British streamlining.

THE JEEP

American Austin Co. in collaboration with the US Army 1940

Alongside *Coca-Cola*, *Wrigleys Gum* and the embellishment of aircraft with a heraldry of Varga and Petty-esque pin-ups, the Jeep embodies the image of the World War II American fighting forces.

Not since the great medieval armourers had military hardware been designed with such a close affinity between function and style, except that the Jeep – being twentieth century and, above all, American – was non-elitist. Soldiers from Eisenhower and Patton down to humble GI Joes (and, on film, John Wayne and countless Hollywood heroes) looked equally at home riding the vehicle which could, as occasion demanded, be a humble workhorse or the white knight's charger. Its rugged functionalism, especially its ability to cope with extremes of terrain and climate, has set a standard for military as well as civilian off-road vehicles ever since.

Yet despite its uniquely American character, the Jeep owed its origins to the British Austin Company (who were in turn to produce their military 4 × 4 field car, the *Champ*) which had introduced an Americanized version of the Austin saloon car into the USA in 1929. Styled by Alexis de Sakhnoffsky to suit the more sophisticated American tastes, and manufactured by the American Austin Company, the car enjoyed brief popularity as a novelty vehicle, particularly amongst the Hollywood crowd. Insufficient sales led to the company going bankrupt in 1934, and it was bought by Ron Evans, who commissioned Sakhnoffsky to restyle the car, which was now made and marketed by the newly-formed Bantam Automobile Company.

Despite its novelty value (a *Bantam* led the New York World's Fair opening parade in 1939 and *Bantams* were used in promotions by companies including Coca-Cola and Firestone) sales were as disappointing as they had been for the original Austin model. *Bantam*'s only rival for the small car market, the *Crosley*, had also been featured in the World's Fair, alongside other Crosley products including radios and refrigerators. Crosley were attempting to fill the gap left by Ford's move away from basic motoring with their 'forgotten man's car', and this was emphasized by its being exhibited with Crosley's consumer appliances in the Communications section of the Fair whilst other automobile manufacturers naturally congregated in the Transportation section. The *Crosley* was cheaper ($65 less than the *Bantam*'s price of $390) and was to be marketed by department stores as well as auto dealers.

The more robust *Bantam* had found favour with the Pennsylvania National Guard for use in field operations, and from this usage came the inspiration for a small military runabout. With the likelihood of American involvement in World War II focusing attention on the neglect of military requirements since the First World War, there was a flurry of military design activity. By mid 1940 the US Army had worked out specifications for a General Purpose vehicle (GP — hence *Jeep*), the most important of which were that its four-wheel drive could accommodate rough terrain, that it could be capable of very low speeds, could take a 500 pound payload and weigh in at no more than 1,300 pounds. Of the hundred companies whose bids to supply such a vehicle were solicited, only Bantam and Willys responded.

Although Willys was only just recovering from the disastrous effects of the Depression, which had virtually wiped out sales for its low budget *Whippet* model and had resulted in its being in receivership between 1933 and 1937, it could offer vast production facilities (in the late twenties it had been America's third largest automobile manufacturing company) as well as talented engineers and designers, many of whom had joined from Chrysler when Joseph Frazer, an ex-Chrysler man, had become President of Willys in 1939.

Bantam, on the other hand, could claim to have initiated the concept of the Jeep with the Pennsylvania National Guard scout car, and with its 1940 prototype meeting all the Army's requirements it was awarded the contract. Unable, however, to meet the production target of 75 vehicles a

Since its first appearance in World War II the US Army Jeep has emanated a certain rugged glamour, and is still charged with associations which even now are powerful enough to warrant a modern reproduction.

day, Bantam lost exclusive rights to Ford and Willys, who eventually produced some 650,000 whilst Bantam, having made only 3,000, went over to trailer production. Willys also contributed its engine, a modified development of its sturdy, four cylinder unit which, though instrumental in the company's original decline (even economy Fords had gone over to six cylinder) had now come into its own. Official recognition of Bantam's role was given in a statement by the Federal Trade Commission: 'the idea of creating the Jeep was originated by the American Bantam Company of Butler, Pennsylvania, in collaboration with certain officers in the United States Army.'

In spite of this, and even in spite of a court injunction to prevent Willys from claiming any more than having contributed to the Jeep's development, *Willys* became the generic wartime term for the Jeep. After the war the Jeep became the design model for the *Landrover*, which then evolved into a unique vehicle in its own right, whilst Willys themselves capitalized on their wartime fame by introducing a Jeep-inspired station wagon, and currently, in the wake of a recent craze for four-wheel-drive Jeep-derived vehicles, the original *Willys* is now back in production, being manufactured in India by the Mahindra Company of Bombay. Though the engine is now a Peugeot one, this modern copy recreates the World War II image even to the extent of its army paintwork, including US insignia, wing-mounted jerry can and a shovel and axe strapped to its side. Though this cannot be regarded as an endorsement of the original design (which proved itself in practice during the war which had initiated it and afterwards), it is nevertheless an indication of the permanent impact of the Jeep's image ■

THE K3 KETTLE

Burrage and Boyd Ltd
1946

As a showcase for post-war British design, the 1946 'Britain Can Make It' Exhibition was naturally compromised by the state of industry still recovering from war-related materials and production problems. The surplus of aluminium, much of which was recycled from scrapped aircraft (itself a highly symbolic process, which was exploited for peace-time 'swords into ploughshares' propaganda), was evidenced in tools and domestic equipment, the section of the exhibition which, as was pointed out in *Design 46* (the book which served as its catalogue), most highlighted the social changes which were occurring.

Reviewing the domestic appliances section Jane Drew saw a 'new orderliness in British design and a seemliness imposed by austerity', and commented that 'our poverty has helped us to avoid many of the vulgarities of pre-war styling, such as bogus streamlining'. If 'bogus' is taken to mean streamlining as a styling exercise rather than for a functional role, the most distinctive item on show was bogus, for Burrage and Boyd's aluminium kettle exemplifies streamline aesthetics to a degree which makes it one of the most outstanding examples of post-Bel Geddes's *Horizons* modernism. The *K3* kettle was marketed as part of the *Picquot Ware* range of aluminium domestic items, which included a serving tray, coffee and tea pots, sugar bowl and cream jug, and remained in production until recently. Despite the fact that its lines derived from pre-war design thinking, like the *Parker 51* the *K3* has taken on a timeless quality, a fact recognized by its inclusion in the 1958 Brussels exhibition as an example of contemporary design ■

Although it never achieved a mass market, the *K3* Kettle, together with the rest of the Picquot Ware range, continued in production long after streamline aesthetics had ceased to be fashionable.

THE LAND CAMERA

Dr Edwin Land 1947

The *Polaroid* camera was first demonstrated by its inventor, Dr Edwin Land, to the Optical Society of America in 1947. The innovation of instant photography made possible by microelectrics exemplified Land's ideal of an inventor's role: 'the duty of the inventor to build a new gestalt and to quietly substitute that gestalt for the old one in the framework of society. And when he does his invention calmly and equitably becomes part of everyday life and no one can understand why it wasn't always there.'

To put the camera into marketable form the obvious choice was Walter Dorwin Teague, who, having already pursued a successful career as a commercial illustrator and typographer, had moved into industrial design in 1927. A year later he began a fruitful association with Eastman Kodak which would produce such memorable cameras as the 1930 stylized art deco *1A Gift* camera, which featured decorative enamel work, the 1934 *Baby Brownie*, which in contrast had a utility bakelite case and sold for only one dollar (four million were sold, making it an outstanding example of product design for the masses) and the 1936 *Bantam Special*. The first *Polaroid*, the *Model 95*, went on the market in 1948 and had, of necessity, a somewhat improvised appearance. In 1954 a new model, the *Model 80*, not only had an improved design but was now cheaper.

In 1961, when the *Polaroid* was redesigned by Albrecht Goertz, it lost its old-fashioned bellows look in favour of a more conventional small-camera form. Goertz's model, the *J66*, was then redesigned by Henry Dreyfuss as the *Model 100*. In 1972 new technology allowed for an instant colour picture which would self-develop without a special pack. The *Model SX-70* took the form of a fold-down camera and was the last design project undertaken by Henry Dreyfuss before his death ■

The old-fashioned looking camera bellows belied the advanced technology of polaroid photography.

LONDON TRANSPORT

The 1948 book *Design at Work*, produced jointly by the Royal Society of Arts and the Council of Industrial Design, described London Transport design as 'essentially practical, impersonal and English. Following no conscious style, it has a timeless quality which makes it a living idiom. Efficiency in operation and ease of maintenance are given first consideration. Architecture and equipment are functionally simple and co-operation between engineer, architect and designer has given a consistency throughout the entire design.'

This appraisal now belongs in the distant past, if only by virtue of the fact that the organization, an integrated metropolitan transport system, no longer exists as an entity, its buses now being run by regional companies and no longer even unified by the red livery which had until recently made them internationally known, whilst the underground system, to the dismay of conservationists, and out of the very real need to improve safety standards, as well as to extend the lives of stations without extensive rebuilding, has undergone a drastic, if inconsistent rehabilitation programme. Nostalgia for the golden years of London Transport, the 1930s, should be tempered with a recognition that the volume of passengers carried was considerably lower, as were running costs, particularly wages – and such social problems as violence and vandalism were yet to come. The London Passenger Transport Board itself was created as a public corporation in 1933, amalgamating the underground with the London General Omnibus Company. Under the directorship of Frank Pick it became a patron of modern architecture, graphics and industrial design.

Architecture

Although the underground never achieved the same unique distinction which Hector Guimard's organic, art nouveau cast iron entranceways brought to the Paris Metro (1898–1901), or the luxurious grand hotel image of the Moscow system, it nevertheless became identified by its

Although now lost to modernization, the bronze columns of the escalator up- lighters (dramatically seen here at Holborn Station), were characteristic of London Transport's house style during the thirties.

Charles Holden's Arnos Grove Station (1932): the acme of London Transport architecture.

buildings, the design ethos of which was echoed in interior details such as booking offices, lighting and seating. The opportunity for new stations came with the rapid expansion of London into the suburbs in the late twenties and thirties. The style is typified by Charles Holden's design for Arnos Grove, whose drum structure has been singled out by Nikolaus Pevsner as 'perhaps more impeccably satisfactory than any other'. Holden, who first worked for Pick in 1924, had researched in Germany, Holland, Denmark and Sweden, absorbing a general feeling rather than any single specific influence. Other than his work for London Transport, Holden is best known for his London University buildings of 1931.

Underground Map

H. C. Beck

Under Pick the London Passenger Transport Board became a patron of the graphic arts, not only through using famous artists for its posters, but also in the less obvious information notices. In 1933 H. C. Beck reduced the map of the underground to a simple, colour-coded chart. Although the information has been subsequently updated, Beck's work remains the textbook example of information graphics.

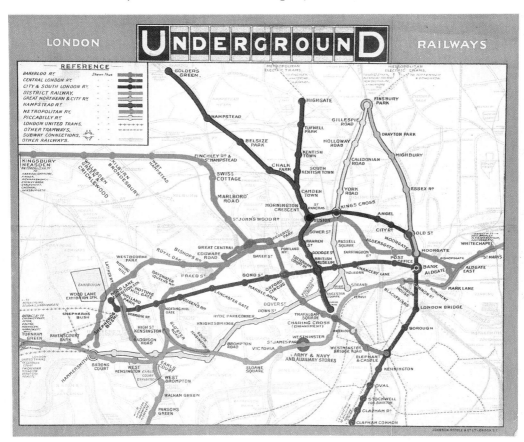

The Routemaster Bus

Douglas Scott and
Eric Ottoway 1954

Beck's tube map was criticized for falsifying the geographical relationship of the stations. However it could be easily updated as new lines were added.

The 1954 *Routemaster* bus was designed specifically for London Transport by Douglas Scott in conjunction with the engineer Eric Ottoway, and is now regarded as the most successful public service road vehicle ever produced. Its principal triumph was achieving a low weight of seven tons without compromising passenger comfort. Douglas Scott, who had originally trained as a silversmith and jeweller before becoming an industrial designer, working in Raymond Loewy's London office before the war, carried on London Transport's style tradition in the use of fabrics and ribbed teak flooring, whilst Scott's engineering produced both reliability and ease of maintenance ∎

The
Routemaster
bus is still seen
as the most
successful
public service
vehicle ever
devised.

LUCKY STRIKE CIGARETTES

Raymond Loewy 1940

Ramond Loewy considered his design for the *Lucky Strike* packet one of the highlights of his long and illustrious career and made frequent anecdotal references to it in his writings and talks, including that given to the Royal Designers for Industry in 1980 when he refuted the critics who had made him out to be a 'temperamental prima donna' by implying that the new *Lucky* pack was dashed off in a theatrical gesture.

The grounds for any such criticism, however, could only have been Loewy's weakness for self publicity, which had revealed how the commission took the form of a $50,000 bet with George Washington Hill, President of American Tobacco, that he could not improve on the traditional *Lucky* package. This should be seen in the context that by then (March 1940) *Lucky* was one of the most popular brands of cigarette, selling over a million packs a year, and had retained the same package since its introduction in 1917. This design consisted of a red target on a deep emerald green background, with the brand name across it. The design appeared on only one side of the pack. Superficially, in terms of its simple elegance and proven market identity, it was already a classic.

Loewy relates that an hour after Hill had left his office his chauffeur returned to deliver a carton of *Luckies* with a card from Hill: 'Put this under your pillow and pleasant dreams'. Two weeks later he presented it to Hill together with the redesigned pack, thereby winning the bet. The green background was now replaced by white, eliminating the problem of the smell of the green ink, which had to be neutralized chemically to avoid tainting the cigarettes and which thus added unnecessary costs to the packaging. Against a white background the target motif became more legible, particularly in a poor light when it had previously been muted against the green. The target now appeared on both sides of the pack, doubling its exposure. Eliminating the green gave *Lucky Strike* a famous wartime advertising slogan – 'Green has gone to war' – which claimed that the bronze used in the green ink was now applied to the war effort.

When folklore surrounds a design exercise, as in the case of the *Lucky* pack, the romantic aura spices history but leaves some unanswered questions. In 1940 the United States was not yet restricting the use of materials in industry to go onto a war footing, so it would appear that dropping the green was not the patriotic gesture which American Tobacco would claim but rather a coincidence which they could exploit in advertising. Their decision to approach Loewy was less likely to have been

Both Loewy's self-promotion and the intensive marketing of the product have made the *Lucky Strike* pack a cult graphic image.

the casual challenge which Loewy relates, but rather part of the general design awareness of American industry at that time which had been particularly highlighted by the strong presence of industrial design in the 1939 World's Fair. Irrespective of its background, the Loewy *Lucky* pack produced an instant 17% increase in sales, and has now surpassed the original in terms of longevity, justifying its own special place in packaging history ■

McDONALD'S

Richard McDonald
1948

Although fast food restaurants are normally perceived as either 'pop' design or a form of commercial folk art, McDonald's pioneered the concept of the designed hamburger chain in two ways: firstly, the rationalized self-service with restricted menu, and secondly, the corporate image.

Richard and Maurice McDonald had operated a successful drive-in 'car hop' restaurant in which customers' orders were brought out to their cars. Mounting labour costs and the concept of self-service, which was beginning to appear in the new supermarkets, prompted the brothers to open the first self-service fast food restaurant in 1948. In order to reduce the operation to a minimum, the menu was restricted to basics, with, in direct contrast to the normal, no options as to dressings and relishes. Thus were the McDonalds introducing twin heresies, offering less service and less choice. In compensation, the savings were passed on to the customer in low prices. Even so, it initially seemed that the brothers had seriously miscalculated as motorists sat outside in their cars, belligerently sounding their horns to summon non-existent car hops. The exceptionally fast service and low prices, however, soon convinced the public that it was worth the effort to get out of their cars and walk up to the service window, and by 1952 McDonald's self-service drive-in was sufficiently successful to attract imitators. The next stage was to establish a corporate identity, essential for the setting up of a franchise operation.

The intuitive marketing instincts of Richard McDonald have resulted in one of the world's most familiar corporate identities.

The value of corporate identity was already being established by Loewy in his designs for the Lucky Stores, a pioneering self-service supermarket, in 1945. Although there already existed a folk-art pop-design aesthetics for hamburger restaurants, which ranged from the traditional rail-car diner style through to Looney Tunes fantasies, such as the famous Brown Derby, there had not yet emerged the fusion of strands of modern architecture with a strong element of kitsch which is now known by Thomas Hine's descriptive label, 'populuxe'. Failing to enlist any architects to realize his vision, Richard McDonald himself designed the prototype, including the famous parabolic arches or, as they became known, the golden arches. An architect commissioned to do the technical work on McDonald's concept is quoted by Philip Langdon in *Orange Roofs, Golden Arches* as stating: 'The colors, the arches were asked for by the McDonalds. The red-and-white striped tile was something they wanted. . . . Dick McDonald was not interested in professional design services. He felt all he needed was someone to translate it to paper.'

Although later the arches were slightly restyled, and eventually became a logo rather than an architectural statement, losing the neon illumination that had given them their garish night-time quality, and though by the mid sixties McDonald's was no longer a simple drive-in but had evolved into a sit-down eatery as well, the global spread of this fast food giant vindicates the McDonald brothers' intuitive innovations ■

THE MINI

Sir Alex Issigonis 1959

The *Mini* represents a landmark in automobile history. Although there already existed many examples of uniquely designed small cars, such as the Citroën *2CV*, the Volkswagen *Beetle* and the Fiat *500* (as well as a profusion of unsuccessful attempts such as the American *Crosley*) Britain's best-selling small car, the British Motor Corporation's *Morris Minor*, which had first appeared in 1948 (and which was destined to have a further fourteen years' production ahead of it when the decision to replace it was made in 1957) was in effect a scaled-down family saloon. By 1957 it was nevertheless showing its age with its distinctive forties jelly-mould profile. The fuel shortage of 1956 resulting from the Suez Crisis had seen the return of petrol rationing and the *Minor*, with a rather antiquated engine, was not particularly economical. Furthermore, the mid fifties had seen a turning point in the British consumer's perceptions, and though the early *Mini* was basic in its interior fittings, had sliding instead of winding windows and wire door-pulls instead of internal handles, it represented a new confidence in British design which would come to fruition during the sixties, an age in which the *Mini* blossomed as a chic symbol of 'swinging' Britain, as well as appearing as a performance sports car or, if customized by Wood and Pickett, a luxury compact.

Sir Alex Issigonis, who had designed the original 1948 *Minor* and who had become BMC's chief engineer in 1951, had been given a 'blank cheque' design brief to produce the new *Minor.*

By having the efficient 848 cc engine mounted transversely, coupled to front wheel drive, the *Mini Minor* was reduced to only ten feet in length, yet had sufficient space to accommodate four people. A further innovation were the ten-inch wheels; the road vibration which these would normally produce was offset by all-independent rubber cone suspension which had

Sir Alex Issigonis's radical approach produced in the *Mini* a new concept in economy motoring – one which soon took on the glamour of a performance sports car as well as the chic of sixties London.

been developed by Dr Alec Moulton, whose research company, Moulton Developments, founded in 1956, had been sponsored in vehicle suspension research by BMC and Dunlop.

Although longevity in itself cannot be the sole yardstick by which the value of a design is to be judged, for it can also be the result of a manufacturer's unwillingness to invest in new design and production expenses, the *Mini*'s phenomenal success since its introduction in 1959, and the fact that nostalgia alone does not account for its having been recently remarketed in a similar form to the original, together with its having set the standard for compacts, elevate the *Mini* to the motoring Hall of Fame ■

THE MINOX CAMERA

Walter Zapp 1937

The end of the last and beginning of this century saw a craze for 'spy' cameras, including such eccentricities as Herman Casler's *Presto* camera – manufactured by E. B. Koopman of New York in 1896 – which looked like an alarm clock, the bizarre hat cameras of J. De Keck of Brussels, Adams of London and Ludus of Görlitz, and the 1910 *Monocular* by H. Roussel of Paris, which was reintroduced in a similar form as the *Ergo* by Zeiss Ikon in 1924.

One of the most successful of these early examples was the *Ticka* of 1903 which was shaped like a watch with the lens cap being a dummy winder. The *Ticka* took 25 pictures on 16mm roll film. In 1937 the *Minox*, designed by Walter Zapp, was first produced by a Lithuanian company, VEF. Like the *Ticka*, the *Minox* used 16mm roll film which was wound on by a simple sliding movement of the telescopic case which has been adopted for the Olympus *XA* camera. Every tiny inch a spy camera, even the lanyard was calibrated so it could be used to measure focal lengths for document copying. The *Minox* continued to be popular as a pocket camera until recently, when the inconvenience of its uncommon film and the availability of small, sophisticated compacts finally made it obsolete ■

The *Minox* was actually issued to spies, as well as enjoying a spell of popularity as a chic pocket camera, until overtaken by new technology.

THE MOKA EXPRESS COFFEE JUG

Renato and Alfonso
Bialetti 1939

Much pre-war Italian industrial design was produced by small workshop manufacturers, a factor which was reflected in the high proportion of craft or low-volume items which were featured in the first post-war showcase of Italian design, the 'Italy at Work' Exhibition.

The *Moka Express* coffee jug was one such low production item. Designed by Renato and Alfonso Bialetti in 1939, its angular, faceted lines typify industrial art deco. Still in production, though on a mass scale, the *Moka* continues to be one of the most successful coffee-making devices, its distinctive lines perpetuating its thirties style without making it appear archaic ■

The *Moka Express* is still in production, its simple practicality and commercial success making it a living design classic.

THE MOULTON BICYCLE

Dr Alex Moulton 1962

The unique design of the *Moulton* bicycle has been somewhat obscured by the inferior copies which resulted from its popularity during the sixties — popularity which had the unfortunate effect of making the bike, despite its advantages over conventional ones, a period piece. That the *Moulton* has not successfully re-emerged during the recent popularity of the bicycle for urban transport — which, despite the *Moulton*'s proven abilities as a rough road and even racing bike, is how it was most used originally — is due more to a shift in fashion than any practical advantages of either the lightweight racing machines or heavy-duty mountain bikes currently in vogue. However, the *Moulton*, like the *Mini-Moke*, was chic in the sixties and now appears to have been relegated to history. Nevertheless, the *Moulton* remains an outstanding example of design engineering, representing a fundamental re-evaluation of the bicycle, to the extent that its most enduring contribution may have been in breaking the stranglehold of tradition on bicycle design. After *Moulton*, these traditions could no longer be sacrosanct.

The *Moulton* bicycle was the product of Dr Alex Moulton's lifelong fascination with bikes — a fascination which he was in an ideal position to exploit thanks to an engineering background which included aeronautical engineering, and to having developed in his own research laboratory the *Flexitor* rubber spring and hydroelastic suspension, which was first used in the 1962 *BMC 1100.*

The *Moulton* was the result of a total reanalysis of the bicycle, in the course of which every previous assumption was challenged and a new shape was created.

As it was a self-initiated project *Moulton* had no restrictions on his fundamental revision of the bicycle, so, for example, his initial research included investigations as to whether the conventional sitting position was in fact superior to reclining. The distinctive open frame was designed to make it the first unisex bicycle, and, with the small wheels, fitted with special high-pressure tyres, it made mounting easy. The small wheels (an idea adopted from the *Mini*) were an essential feature and although several plagiarists approximated them by using the wheels of junior bikes, those of the *Moulton* were specially made, an example of Moulton's attention to detail, for he had determined that his prototype should be fully developed (as he put it, 'immaculate') before soliciting manufacturers.

In the event, the conservative attitude of the bicycle industry found Moulton's design too innovative, obliging him to manufacture and market it himself. Although the actual production was eventually carried out by a division of the British Motor Corporation, a combination of poor quality

control and a glut of inferior imitations (which, lacking Moulton's combination of special wheels and suspension, gave an inferior perform-ance that tarnished the small-wheel concept including, undeservedly, the *Moulton*) effectively killed off the *Moulton*). Although a new, redesigned *Moulton* appeared in the 1980s, the classic original seems destined to remain forever identified with the sixties ■

THE OLIVETTI LETTERA 22 TYPEWRITER

Olivetti's *Lettera*

Marcello Nizzoli 1950 *22* typewriter of 1950, designed by Marcello Nizzoli, became the definitive portable, characterized by its lightweight construction and minimalist compactness. Nizzoli had been chief designer for Olivetti since 1936, in which capacity he had been responsible for the *MC45 Summa* adding machine. After the war, Nizzoli's *Lexicon 80* of 1948 was amongst the products which signalled Italy's re-entry into international industrial design, being featured in the 'Italy at Work' Exhibition held at the Art Institute of Chicago in 1950. The *Lettera 22* was awarded the Compasso d'Oro at the 10th Triennale in 1954. Nizzoli redesigned the replacement for the *Lexicon 80*, the *Diaspron* in 1959, introducing a new, hard-edged look which was to be further developed by Ettore Sottsass in the 1964 *Teckne 3* ■

Olivetti were pioneer patrons of industrial design, producing several historical landmarks, including the award winning *Lettera 22*.

THE OSTERIZER BLENDER

Don Carlson and Al
Madl 1953

The electric blender was first introduced in 1937 by the Waring Mixer Corporation. In 1945 it was redesigned by Francesco Collura, who accentuated the base with vertical ribs which encroached onto the glass beaker top, emphasizing not only that the top was secure but also that the blender would not topple over. In 1948 it was again redesigned by Peter Müller-Munk who removed the ribbing, leaving only locating spurs at the top, and increased the base area so that the base tapered upwards in a series of steps. The success of this blender has prompted its re-introduction.

Another classic blender, the 1953 *Osterizer*, has also returned onto the market. Designed by Don Carlson and Al Madl, the *Osterizer Model 403* shares with the Müller-Munk a characteristic, heavy chromed base — though in this case the stepping is soft form rather than hard edged — and an extremely chunky glass top. Despite being designed for the domestic market, both now have the feel of professional catering equipment, which gives them a contemporary high-tech image ■

The *Osterizer* blender has returned to the market, not as an archaic 'retro classic' but because it is a design which is still commercially viable.

P

THE PARKER 51

Marlin Baker, Joseph
Platt and Kenneth
Parker 1939

The *Parker 51* was, and is probably destined to remain, the definitive modern fountain pen. Throughout the thirty-seven years it was in production (1940–1977) it represented the epitome of elegance, transcending its original status as the embodiment of modern Streamline by becoming a timeless classic.

It was introduced in 1939 and named in celebration of the fifty-first anniversary of George Parker's first marketing a fountain pen of his own design and manufacture. Of greater historical significance, however, it was also the year of the New York World's Fair, the climax of what has been described as the 'Streamline Decade' and a showcase for the recent rise to pre-eminence which the American industrial designers were enjoying.

Although its sleek contours are redolent of Streamline, the *51* was much more than a styling exercise. Its innovative technology was eventually eclipsed by the ball-point (patented the year before the *51* was introduced but not in general use until the fifties), whilst memories of the mess which, prior to the *51*, had characterized the fountain pen faded over the years, and a new generation who had never experienced it arrived. The new technology of the *51* was not solely in the pen itself, but also in the ink, whose development had necessitated the pen. This ink had special properties which enabled it to soak into the paper, doing away with the blotting process which had been a feature of conventional ink which dried through evaporation. The new fast-drying ink was unsuitable for standard pens, and dictated several elements of the *51* which are often assumed to be merely styling. For example, its viscosity would have caused it to flood a conventional nib, a problem which the *51* overcame by incorporating a small reservoir under the nib into which an accumulation of excess drains. This reservoir is concealed by the cutaway hood which shields all but the tip of the nib, and which, by doing away with the nib as a dominant feature, makes possible the *51*'s distinctively uncluttered sleekness.

Both its sophisticated technology and styling made the *Parker 51* one of the first cult consumer objects.

There are other instances of the relationship between technology and style. The *51*'s squeeze-action ink sac dispensed with the traditional lever, allowing the pen's smoothness to be unflawed. Even its use of the new plastic, Lucite, was dictated by the ink, one characteristic of which was that it corroded Pyralin, the hard rubber-derived material of which most pens were made.

The *51* was the work of Marlin Baker, Joseph Platt and Kenneth Parker, and represented, together with the ink, some quarter of a million dollars in development costs; it was, from the start, a designed pen. Although his contributions are not specified, Moholy-Nagy, who became a design consultant to Parker in 1939, a role which encompassed every aspect of the company's products, including packaging, was certainly involved in the development of the *51*, as is shown in this extract from an article he wrote in Parker's house magazine a few months before his death in 1946: 'The *51* pen is one of the most successful designs of small utility objects in our period. It is light, handy, extremely well shaped, unobtrusive and perfectly functional. Now that the cap is changed and simplified, I am only waiting for the acceptance of a more appropriate Parker arrow clip and then my delight will be complete. When I first came to the Parker Pen Company it was often thought that my duties were to style and fashion the products which the Research and Development Department considered as well engineered. Slowly, however, they yielded to my curiosity as to the mechanical functions of the product and they were willing to take suggestions if I could offer any improvement, not only of the appearance, but of its function.'

From its inception the *51* was a cult object, and may even have been the first consumer product to achieve that status. Its high price (in 1940 its price was $12.50, the equivalent of about £80 today) and the fact that world demand exceeded production enhanced its desirability, and Parker's publicity quickly exploited such newsworthy stories as the Chinese Government awarding *51*s instead of medals to deserving citizens and the use of a *51* by General Bedell Smith, Eisenhower's Chief of Staff when he signed the instrument of surrender on behalf of the allies in May 1945. Although celebrity endorsements continued to feature in Parker's marketing, the pen's success owed little to hype. In 1959 it was voted the fourth best designed consumer product of modern times by American Architects and Designers (an honour it shared with Loewy's '53 *Studebaker Coupé*). Top of the list had been the Olivetti *Lettera 22*, followed by an Eames chair and the *Barcelona* chair, design classics with which the *51* can still be regarded as a near equal ■

PENGUIN BOOKS

Edward Young 1935

Penguin books, the brainchild of the publisher Allen Lane, first appeared in 1935, and can be regarded as products of the climate of that time, in which benevolent social ideals motivated new concepts in design and marketing. There are similarities between the ethos of Penguin – broadly, entertainment and culture for the masses presented through modern design – and the causative link between the style of the BBC and radio sets of the time.

The idea that the general public should buy good books rather than borrow them from libraries was in itself revolutionary, and even a quarter of a century later Mr Mervyn Griffith-Jones, prosecuting Penguin on an obscenity charge for publishing D. H. Lawrence's *Lady Chatterley's Lover*, could introduce the class element into his argument by pointing out that the paperback was affordable and that even a servant could read it.

Although by the mid thirties an increase in adult literacy was already apparent, the high price of conventionally published books restricted the majority of readers either to buying cheap abridged editions through stores like Woolworths or borrowing from the 'tuppenny' lending libraries. Not only the price but the way books were sold intimidated many, as Allen Lane explained at the time in an article in *The Bookseller*: 'Their fears are twofold; firstly, of their financial liability . . . ; secondly, their ignorance. They feel at home in a tuppenny library or at Woolworths, where they get the same amount of attention if they spend five shillings or if they go out with nothing at all; but the idea of braving an empty bookshop with two or three assistants lying in wait behind the shelves is too much for them. Penguin Books are designed primarily to reach the people, where they congregate on railway stations and chain stores, with the hope that when they see these books are available in the regular bookshops they will overcome their temerity and come in.'

That Lane should refer to design is significant, for it is present in every aspect of the books. Sold for sixpence, they automatically came within the symbolic top price set by Woolworths, where nothing was supposed to cost more than that (although this was sometimes a spurious limit achieved, for example, by pricing saucepans at sixpence but selling the lids as a separate item for another sixpence).

The fact that a major outlet would be railway bookstalls determined the books' size (a contemporary article noted that they were 'just the right size and weight for squeezing in pockets and tucking in rucksacks and offer ideal holiday reading'), but the innovative use of monotype, at a time when most cheap printing was set in linotype, and the good quality paper ensured that despite the compact format the print was highly legible. In addition to being of uniform size, the appearance of the books was standardized, a house style being an essential part of marketing. Designed by Edward Young, who was also responsible for the Penguin logo, the books were spartan compared with the garish pictures and jumbled typography which had previously characterized cheap publications.

The books' covers gave the title and author's name, using a variety of sizes of Monotype Sans (designed by Eric Gill between 1928 and 1930) on a white background. At the top and bottom of this white band, colour was used as a code to the nature of the book so that, for example, green signified 'Murder and Mystery'. The clarity of the titles and the colour coding were both essential to Penguin's marketing, facilitating the hurried selection made at a station bookstall and assisting the intimidated potential readers Lane alluded to.

The first *Penguin*, *Ariel* by the French writer André Maurois, was immediately followed by nine others, including Ernest Hemingway's *A Farewell to Arms* and Agatha Christie's *The Mysterious Affair at Styles*. Although Lane's motives were generally applauded, many literary figures, including George Orwell, saw the paperback as a threat to the lending libraries and the publishing of new work. Despite these misgivings, the success of Penguin was established beyond doubt when three million were sold in the first year ■

Penguin's standardized format, colour coding and recognizable house style were part of a marketing strategy to take the mystique out of book buying.

THE PENGUIN POOL, LONDON ZOO

Berthold Lubetkin and
Tetron 1938

The coincidental link between the penguin's black-and-white plumage and man's formal evening dress brings to the London Zoo's Penguin Pool the atmosphere of a 1930s film musical. That the pool has the air of being a set is, however, no coincidence, for its designers, Lubetkin and the Tetron Group, had been briefed by Sir Peter Chalmers-Mitchell, the zoo's director, that it should be a showcase for the penguins, giving maximum scope for their natural tendency to congregate in groups, as well as providing surfaces to dive from and a large swimming area. Without becoming embroiled in the issues of the moral rightness of zoos in general, it is notable that this represented a new humane attitude to the zoo's exhibits, an attitude which was reflected in the choice of Lubetkin, who though responsible for other zoo buildings, most notably at Whipsnade and Dudley, is chiefly known for his strong social commitment, exemplified in his Finsbury Health Centre and his proposed, but never realized, *Project for Working Class Flats*. A contemporary article on the Pool published in *Mother and*

The theatrical presentation of London Zoo's penguins was achieved through sophisticated structural engineering and Berthold Lubetkin's humanitarianism.

Child magazine, November 1938, serves as a poignant reminder that a penguin's environment was superior to that of many humans: 'How many citizens of London have brooded over the railings of that pool, envying the penguins as they streak through the blue water or plod up the exquisite incline of the ramp – and have wondered sadly why human beings cannot be provided, like the penguins, with an environment so well adapted to their needs.'

The publicity which the pool attracted was a factor in widening the acceptability of modern design, and may have thus indirectly contributed towards an improvement in the planning of human environments, a goal which Lubetkin had in mind when designing it. The relatively large scale of the interlocking curved ramps, some 46 feet (14 m) long, and their ethereal thinness (varying between 3 and 6 inches) demonstrated the role of the structural engineer (Ove Arup) in realizing 'the exquisite incline of the ramps', which anticipated motorway flyovers by some quarter of a century. Unfortunately the betterment of the human environment referred to by *Mother and Child* magazine is less apparent, and it was Lubetkin's disillusionment with the political realities of social design which brought about his premature retirement, leaving the penguins among the few direct beneficiaries of his utopian designs ■

■R

THE RIETVELD CHAIR

Gerrit Rietveld 1917

Gerrit Rietveld was not yet a member of the De Stijl group when he designed and made the famous red/blue chair. With a family background of cabinet making, Rietveld had in fact spent his youth in his father's workshop before studying architecture, initially at night school and then in an architect's office. In 1911 he opened his own workshop, but continued to study architecture until 1915. In 1917 he designed the red/blue chair which, as Rietveld was later to state, defined space – the effect being that 'a special segment of space has been absorbed into our human system'. In its original form it differed from the chair that has become so familiar, as at first it had side panels which were only removed at some time after 1919. Nor was it designed with its polychromic finish, which was applied to its original bare wood finish after Rietveld became involved with the De Stijl group.

Although the red/blue chair is now regarded as much as a fine art object as a design exercise, those who have had the opportunity to sit in it report that it is both comfortable and ergonomically sound. It is therefore interesting to speculate how the chair would be regarded had its unique design (as Giedion expressed it 'to forget everything and begin afresh, as if no chair had ever been built') remained in bare wood, and – more significantly – had it gone into the sort of craft mass-production that Rietveld had in mind when he designed its construction to be within the competence of any artisan cabinet maker ■.

Although artificially elevated to the status of fine art, Gerrit Rietveld's chair was originally intended to reach a mass market through production by small cabinet makers.

THE ROLADEX 5024

Arnold Neustadter
and Hildaur Neilson
1958

The rotary card file system was introduced in 1958 by the Roladex Corporation of New Jersey. Designed by the company's President, Arnold Neustadter, and engineer Hildaur Neilson, its chromed tubular frame and bakelite knobs give it a 1920s Bauhaus look. This archaic quality creates the subconscious impression that the *Roladex* has a longer pedigree than it really has. Even though this quality was, no doubt, unintentional, it gives the *Roladex* the appearance of being a design classic by association. Most important is the system's proven practicability which, despite electronic technology, still makes it the most compact desk-top information retrieval system ■

Devoid of sophisticated technology, and somewhat old-fashioned in style, the *Roladex* is still in production as an efficient information retrieval system.

ROSENTHAL STUDIO LINE 2000

By the 1950s the old established German family

Raymond Loewy 1954

firm, Rosenthal, had a reputation for high quality ceramics which, though well designed, tended towards the traditional. The arrival of Philip Rosenthal as marketing manager in 1950 heralded a positive attempt to revive the dynamic image Rosenthal had enjoyed in the thirties. His task was to change the consumer perception of Rosenthal ware as a once-in-a-lifetime purchase – the heirloom factor – and to expand its export market. North America had always been a major importer of European china, which was particularly favoured for the lucrative bridal market. Rosenthal were already an established name in the USA with a distributor network, and the 1949 Museum of Science and Industry New York exhibition of German products had done much to create an atmosphere in which Americans were prepared to put the war behind them and accept German goods. To ensure success, Rosenthal decided to employ an American designer, and Loewy – not only for his proven record but also as an uniquely 'European' American – was the natural choice.

The first Loewy designs, the *E line* and *Undine*, retained a European flavour, but for 1954 the *2000* range (credit for which Loewy cedes to Philip Latham, who was employed by Loewy for his thorough understanding of the technical aspects of ceramics production) achieved a unique style, being regarded as the epitome of modern ceramics when it was launched at the Hanover Trade Fair in 1954. The line continued in production until 1978, with Rosenthal spending vast sums on research and design, with the result that over 150 different applied decorations embellished the range in the course of its life ■

The success of
the *Studio Line*
vindicated
Rosenthal's
decision to use
the Loewy
studio to
expand the
company's
exports in
America.

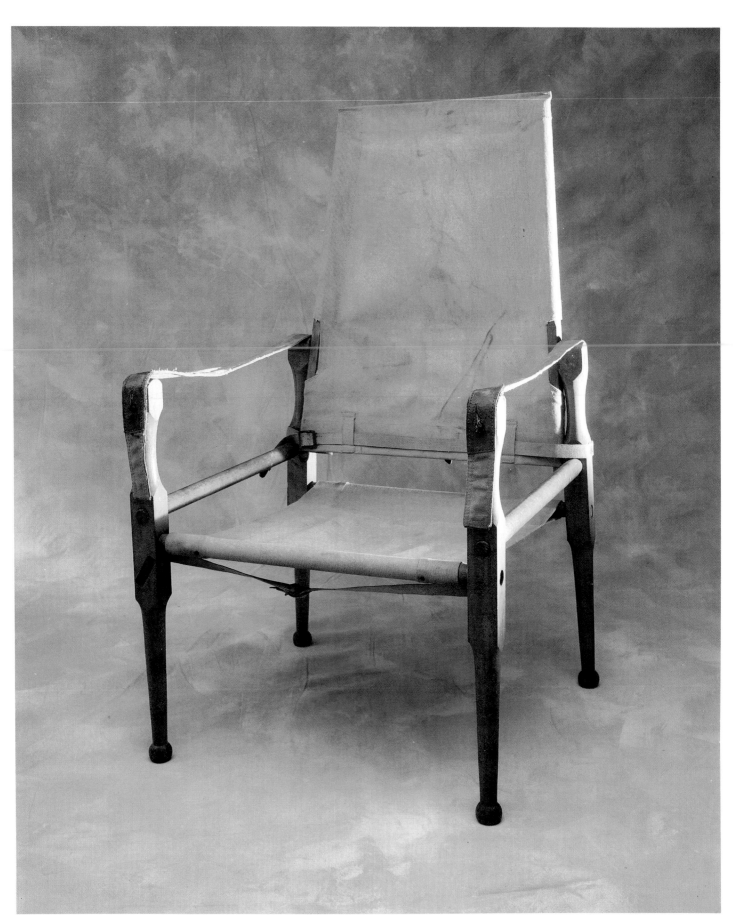

THE SAFARI CHAIR

Kare Klint 1933

So great is the extent to which 20th century design has depended on factors unique to this century — such as new materials and production techniques, marketing and communications, political and social trends — that it has tended towards a repudiation of the past. Even when designers have been conscious of inheriting a craft tradition their work, as in the case of Rietveld's furniture, has usually been new in form despite the use of traditional materials and techniques. In some cases, however, established forms from the past have been adapted to new materials and fabrication techniques; obvious examples include the conceptual link between Thornet's bentwood furniture and the use of tubular steel, and between 19th century moulded papier mâché furniture and 20th century plastic forms.

A major advocate of design as a continuum was the Danish architect Kare Klint, whose father — the painter, engineer and architect, Jensen — is best known for the Grundvig church in Copenhagen, and who was himself an influential teacher in the Furniture School of the Danish Academy of Art, where he championed the study of design history, particularly the work of the 18th century cabinet makers. Like Rietveld, Klint believed that furniture designed for high volume production could be made by numerous small workshops rather than one large factory, resulting in better quality and greater flexibility, as well as ensuring the preservation of the craft tradition.

His most famous design, the 1933 *Safari* chair, is essentially a reworking of a 19th century camping chair. Combining wood, canvas and leather, the chair is designed to come apart as though for travelling, a pedantic link with its 19th century inspiration which demonstrates that the chair exists not only as a piece of 20th century design but also perpetuates a classic from the last century ■

Although this original *Safari* Chair (sold by the Army & Navy Stores in Calcutta) is redolent of British colonialism, Klint's near copy of 1933 revitalized it as a 'modern' design.

SCRABBLE

Alfred Mosher Butts
1938

Although *Scrabble* appears to be quite a simple concept, it is remarkable as being the solution to a self-initiated design problem devised by a New York architect, Alfred Mosher Butts, who had seen a potential market for a game 'with a balance between all skill, like chess, and no skill, like dice'. In 1938, after five years working on it, he had devised the game of *Scrabble*. Following a predictable course of events, Butts's new game was universally rejected by all the manufacturers he solicited, and, again true to the script, he persevered, manufacturing the game himself out of wood as a cottage industry. In 1947 a new attempt was made to market the game, with little success. Five years later, for no discernible reason, and, paradoxically, at a time when television was being accused of dominating leisure and heralding a dark age of illiteracy, sales suddenly took off, quickly reaching one million. Whilst there must be thousands of less happy stories when designers have been unable to vindicate ideas which have been given the thumbs-down, it is heartening that one man's originality, in the form of Butts's *Scrabble* or Hickman's *Workmate*, can beat the system ■

Its popularity undiminished, *Scrabble* represents the triumph of its designer's vision over initial commercial rejection.

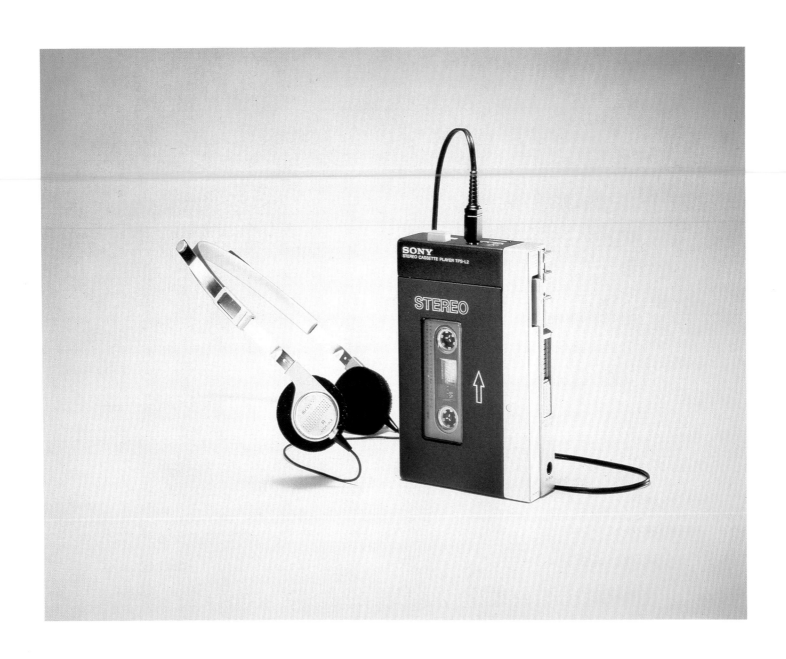

THE SONY WALKMAN

Sony Corporation
1979

In 1955 the Tokyo Tsushin Kogyo Company (TTK) introduced the world's first mass produced transistor radio, the *Sony TR 55* (which inspired TTK to change its name to Sony), followed by the first pocket transistor radio in 1957 and the first portable miniature television in 1959. Even so, Japanese industrial products were seen as technically proficient but otherwise lacking design qualities. This perception is exemplified by the organizers of the 1960 American exhibition 'Japan: Design Today' — which was jointly compiled by the Walker Art Centre, the Smithsonian Institution and the Japanese Export Trade Organization — who concentrated on craft objects, on the basis that 'some of the industrial products, especially cameras and optical equipment, radios, television sets and other electronic equipment, were excellent as products but not outstanding as original contributions to design'.

Although at that time there may have been grounds for this criticism, Sony already had a design section which in 1961 was amalgamated with advertising and product development to achieve a co-ordinated image. In 1979 Sony introduced its most popularly successful design, the *Walkman*. Over two million *Walkmans* were sold within the first eighteen months, establishing it as a cult object which attracted copies, as well as inspiring Sony to produce a series of increasingly sophisticated developments ■

The Sony *Walkman* brought an unexpected novelty to a public who had become blasé about technology, but it was not long before the novelty seemed more like a necessity to young people all round the world.

THE STANLEY KNIFE

Stanley Tools 1936

The idea of the throwaway blade was pioneered in 1895 by King C. Gillette, the first safety razor going into production in 1903. Although the idea eventually reached its logical conclusion with the *Bic*, where the entire razor was disposable, the principle of the throwaway blade was not introduced to the work knife until 1936, when Stanley Tools introduced the *199* utility knife. Although now available in a retractable blade version, the much-imitated *Stanley* knife has remained essentially the same since then, a timeless example of a perfect utility design ■

The practical robustness of the *Stanley* knife has survived minor styling changes: styling does not matter much when the success of the design lies in its functional simplicity.

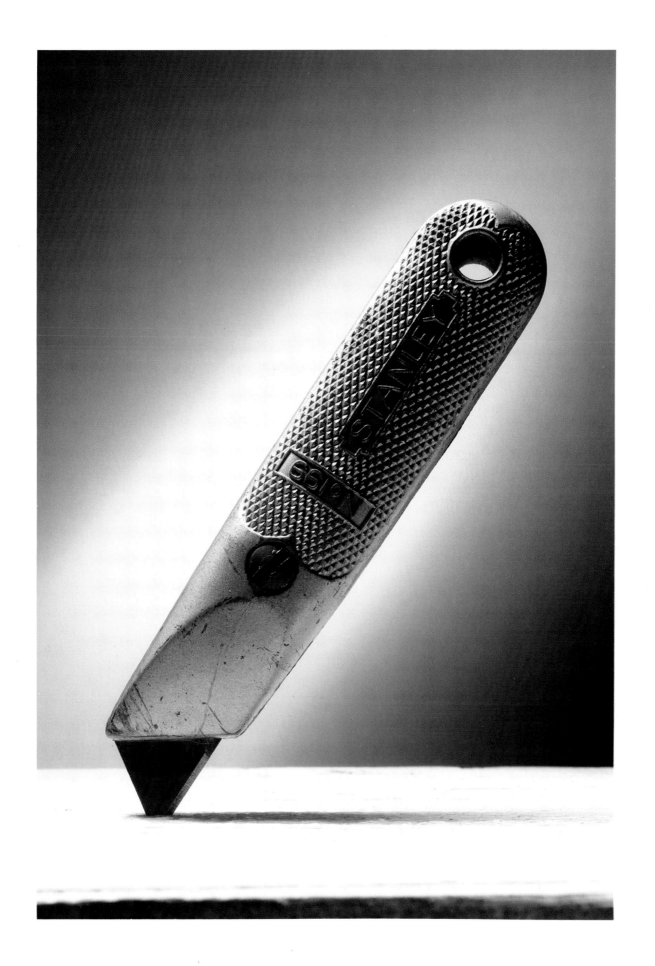

TELEAVIA

Philippe
Charbonneaux
1957

Once it had passed its early small-screen-in-a-cabinet stage, the television was left in a design limbo, the majority of manufacturers, particularly the Americans, being content to emphasize the set's function as luxury home furnishing. Obviously, weight and bulk originally imposed restrictions on design, particularly the depth which was necessary until the advent of the slimline tube. Nevertheless, during the fifties there appeared three radical solutions to the problem of the television being literally 'the box'. All three achieved this through separating the tube from the controls. The Italian *Phonola* set of 1956, designed by Sergio Berizzi, Cesare Butte and Dario Montagni featured a tear-drop-like tube housing on top of a minimalistic box structure mounted on cross-strutted legs. The French *Téléavia* of 1957, designed by Philippe Charbonneaux, had a similarly styled upper structure, and also succeeded in reducing the lower half to a less bulky affair. The American *Predicta* television, made by Philco, introduced in 1958, was even more adventurous in allowing the picture tube, which was linked to the controls by a cable, to be located across the room from the control box, thus crudely anticipating remote control TV. Although the *Predicta* was on the market for several years, it was made obsolete both by slimlines and lightweight portables ■

The screen of the *Téléavia* could be both swivelled and tilted — one of the ingenious attempts to break away from the inert bulk of the conventional set.

THE TIZIO LAMP

Richard Sapper 1972

Although its antecedent is the *Anglepoise* lamp, the connection between the *Anglepoise*'s pedantic articulation and the *Tizio*'s ethereal effortlessness of movement is solely conceptual. Designed by Richard Sapper for the Italian company, Artemide, in 1972, the *Tizio* had the advantage over the *Anglepoise* of advances in lighting technology. The *Anglepoise* used a conventional incandescent light bulb, which in itself is fairly bulky. This bulk in turn dictated the size of the reflector, their combined weight dictating the size and weight of the lamp base. A further disadvantage of the conventional light bulb was that it ran on direct mains current. The diameter of electrical cables is governed not only by the gauge of wire needed to conduct the power, but also by the thickness of the cable's insulation as prescribed for that power. The thickness and lack of flexibility of the *Anglepoise*'s wiring was a further factor in the lamp's relatively chunky construction. In contrast, the *Tizio* used a low-voltage halogen lamp, whose diminutive size not only allowed the reflector area to be compact and lightweight, but also had the advantage of needing only thin and flexible wiring. The small low-voltage transformer was neatly accommodated in the lamp's base, which provided stability with the minimum of bulk. Freed from the necessity of having to counteract both the problems of bulk and inflexible wiring which burdened the *Anglepoise*, the *Tizio*'s slender arms employed counterweights to achieve precise positioning through fingertip control. This effortless action gives the *Tizio* the fascination of an executive toy, whilst its combination of precision engineering and (at the time) novel use of halogen can justify its (perhaps dubious) claim to be the herald of the cult of high-tech design ■

Both
aesthetically
and
technically, the
Tizio's striking
qualities made
it an instant
cult object.

TUPPERWARE

Earl Tupper 1945

The marketing strategy of the 'Tupperware party', which in itself is redolent of 1950s American suburbia, has tended to overshadow the products themselves. Invented and produced by Earl Tupper in 1945, the containers were the result of Tupper's discovery that polythene could be moulded to retain sufficient pliability to enable a lid to snap on tightly enough to exclude air, yet could be easily prised off. A further innovation was Tupper's decision to restrict any decoration to the tinting of the plastic. *Tupperware* products were sold directly to the public by means of the party system from 1951, sales being further assisted by the rapid growth of domestic refrigeration for which the containers proved ideal ■

The marketing strategy of the sales party makes *Tupperware* as much a phenomenon of social history as of design.

THE VENDO 44

The Vendo Company,
Kansas City USA 1956

Like many industrial products, the *Vendo 44 Coca-Cola* bottle vender is the work of anonymous designers, yet it surpasses Loewy's much-vaunted work for Coca-Cola in terms both of functionalism and styling. Indeed, the *Vendo 44*, produced between 1956 and 1959, together with its bigger predecessor, the 1949 *V.39*, represent the acme of Coca-Cola vending machine style.

Its styling quality lies not in anything innovative, but rather in the refinement of existing design ideas into a compact form. Severely old-fashioned, its rounded shoulders and narrow proportions echo pre-war petrol pumps, whilst its lever mechanism gives the customer the element of action which is the traditional way to humanize a machine. Only 16" wide, 15½" deep and 58" high, it can nevertheless hold 44 bottles of *Coke*, nine of which are pre-chilled in readiness for the customer. Whilst their bulk makes many vending machines appear intimidating, the little *44*, its heavy gauge steel case enamelled in bright red with a white top (a feature introduced on vending machines in 1955 to evoke the coldness of the drinks inside) appears to be the definitive user-friendly machine ■

Designed solely to dispense bottled *Coca-Cola*, the *Vendo 44* achieved remarkable compactness – unusual in an age when big generally meant better.

THE VESPA

Corriadino d'Ascando
1946

The *Vespa* motor scooter which, it is claimed, was the real star of the 1953 Gregory Peck movie *Roman Holiday*, a film which did much to popularize the idea of carefree Italian chic, was introduced in 1946. Together with its rival, Innocenti's *Lambretta* and Robiati's domestic espresso coffee machine, it was among the hard industrial items which the American team responsible for the 'Italy at Work' Exhibition discovered amongst the more craft-orientated objects deriving from the immediate post-war *Ricostruzione* period. Designed by Corriadino d'Ascando, the *Vespa* had a slightly futuristic look with its flowing, streamlined body panels enclosing as much as possible of its mechanism; its lightweight monocoque construction revealed its designer's background as an aeronautical engineer. Conceived originally as utility transport, it was an instant success, with 18,000 being produced by Piaggio in the first year. It was an auspicious start to what would be, with minor changes, 41 years of continuous production, during which the *Vespa* achieved a global market, both as an economic form of transport and later also as a cult pleasure vehicle ■

The *Vespa* scooter: still in extensive use in its original, prosaic role as utility transport, as well as being perennially popular for its youthful image.

■V

THE VOLKSWAGEN BEETLE

Dr Ferdinand Porsche
1937

Although banished to Brazil, having been deemed too antiquated to warrant German factory space, the Volkswagen *Beetle* is still in production half a century after it first appeared, a record for car design unlikely to be beaten. The car was originally designed by Dr Ferdinand Porsche in 1937 as an economy, 'people's car' – the equivalent of the *Model T* Ford. Politically, it was an important element in the democratic prosperity of New Germany, and was initially known as the *KdF Wagen* from Dr Robert Ley's Nazi Arbeitsfront motto 'Kraft durch Freude' (strength through joy). With a selling price of only 990 Reichmarks, the *Volkswagen* was as cheap to run as it was to buy, featuring a rear-mounted, air-cooled flat four engine whose short stroke 3,200 r.p.m. could produce a constant top speed of 60 m.p.h. and do 50 miles to the gallon.

The aerodynamic body shape, which owed much to America's experiments in streamlining in the thirties, also contributed to fuel economy. The strict limitations on the selling price demanded by its Third Reich sponsors resulted in some inadequate technical features, most particularly an inferior cable-operated braking system which nevertheless became an idiosyncratic feature of the car for its first twelve years.

At the outbreak of war, production ceased as Volkswagen went over to military vehicles. After the war the car was back under the supervision of the forces of occupation, with some 6,000 being built in 1947. Although the British Army was running Volkswagen in a caretaker capacity – as much as a technical exercise as anything else – it was not one of the assets of the Reich on offer for war reparation which the allies were anxious to acquire. Britain's Lord Rootes reported in 1946, following a visit to the factories, that 'a car like this will remain popular for two or three years, if that. To build the car commercially would be a completely uneconomic enterprise.' The Americans were equally uninterested, their only recognition of the *Volkswagen* appearing in Buick's advertisements – 'Yes, the engine is still up front' – which acknowledged an anxiety American industry was facing, that enough GIs had been exposed to European style to create an unpatriotic backlash against American consumerism.

As it was, the American public's amusement on first seeing a *Volkswagen* seemed to justify Ford's assessment when it had been offered to them that it wasn't 'worth a damn'. The *Volkswagen* was featured in 1948 in an exhibition of German products at the Museum of Science and Industry in New York. To avoid any offence, it had been promised that all the items on show were 'de-Nazified'.

The *Volkswagen* soon began the process of design evolution which was to ensure its survival – a variant on the original was the 1949 *Karman* convertible cabriolet – and the car's spartan image was mitigated by colour, as Volkswagen's customers had originally been given the same

choice as Henry Ford's — 'any colour so long as it's black'. In 1952 the minuscule two-piece rear window lost its dividing strut; it changed to an oval shape in 1956 and was considerably enlarged in 1958. In 1962 the rear lights were enlarged, which, together with the later introduction of impact-absorbing bumpers, only marginally affected the original 1930s aerodynamic profile.

Volkswagen's success in the market place had been steady rather than spectacular, though it did, surprisingly, confound all predictions in America by becoming the David to challenge Detroit's Goliath. By 1958 that heart of the American Consumer Society was already in decline, with sales of some 4.6 million compared with the 1955 peak of 7.9 million. Foreign imports accounted for 7.3% of US car sales, headed by Volkswagen, who outsold both Chrysler and Studebaker. It was undoubtedly this successful challenge to the American automobile industry on its own ground that did much to encourage the development of the Japanese small car.

Paradoxically, the *Beetle* recently (particularly the convertible) enjoyed a cult status which made it the social, if not the technical, equal to Volkswagen's Giorgetto Giugiaro-designed *Golf*, and, just as the *Morris Minor* had continued after the introduction of the *Mini*, so the new and old continued a brief spell of incongruous co-existence. Though like the *Minor* and the *2CV*, much of the *Beetle*'s cult popularity can be attributed to nostalgia, it is also a recognition that a design can embody enduring qualities that long outlive its original purpose ■

Before the emergence of the Japanese car industry, the *Volkswagen* was the first foreign import seriously to challenge the American market.

THE WASSILY CHAIR

Marcel Breuer 1926

Originally, the furniture workshop of the Bauhaus, which was under the directorship of Marcel Breuer, was known as the cabinet-making workshop and was restricted to woodwork, as a result of which Breuer's original experiments in tubular steel furniture in 1925 were not carried out in the Bauhaus itself. The similarity in structure of tubular framed furniture and the bicycle initially prompted Breuer to approach the cycle firm of Adler as potential manufacturers, for he intended it to be mass-produced, and, although never on the scale Breuer had envisaged, the *Wassily* (named in honour of his friend, the artist Wassily Kandinsky) went into production through the Standard-Mobel Company of Berlin in 1926. Other, simpler chairs utilizing the combination of stretched fabric and tubular steel framework were also manufactured by Standard-Mobel, whose advertising claimed that 'due to its durability and sanitary quality Breuer metal furniture is 200 per cent more economical in use than ordinary chairs'. Within a couple of years of the pioneering *Wassily* design, tubular steel furniture was in common use, but Breuer continued to work in wood as well.

Although the *Wassily* chair, as well as variants of Breuer's other tubular steel furniture, is still in production, it was his 1928 cantilevered *Cesca* chair which, albeit often in the form of imitations, fulfilled his ambitions by becoming the mass-produced *Model T* of chairs. Whereas credit for the first successful cantilever chair is given to Mart Stam, Breuer's simple solution of a seat, back and arms bolted onto a tubular frame – as opposed to Stam's chair, where the seat and back are laced onto the frame, or Mies van der Rohe's cantilever, which, like the *Weissenhof* chair, uses wickerwork – proved to be the most practical for manufacture ■

The use of tubular steel not only freed furniture design from traditional limitations of construction, but made mass production possible.

THE WOOLMARK

Francesco Saroglio
1964

Launched in 1964, the Woolmark, a part op-art, part calligraphic rendering of a ball of wool, is a classic example of the international heraldry of the corporate image. The Woolmark was designed by Francesco Saroglio of Milan for the International Wool Secretariat, who used it to spearhead a global $150 million campaign to promote wool against the growing threat of synthetics. Not only was the Woolmark instantly recognizable, it was also truly international by avoiding the written word ■

CERTIFICATION TRADE MARK
PURE NEW WOOL

Internationalism has produced the need for universally recognized symbols, amongst which the *Woolmark* must rank as the most apt graphic image.

THE WORKMATE

Ronald P. Hickman
1961–1971

One of the most amazing things about the *Workmate* is that although it is, in essence, a simple mechanical tool it is a very recent invention. We have become so conditioned to labour-saving devices being the result of sophisticated electronic technology that the purely mechanical functions of the *Workmate* (the apparent simplicity of which belies its engineering qualities) provoke the assumption that this is a modern version of some traditional device. In fact, when it first appeared on the market it was a completely new tool with no historical precedent.

Indeed, it was the very absence of anything providing even the most basic of its functions, that of a portable workbench, which brought it about. Its designer, Ronald P. Hickman, had no formal education in either design or engineering, although this had not prevented his achieving his ambition to be a car designer, joining Lotus cars after working for Ford and being involved in the 1957 *Elite* sports car. In 1962 he became Design Director of Lotus, where he was responsible for the *Elan*, the *Elan + 2*, the *Europa* and the Lotus *Cortina.* In 1961, whilst building some furniture at home, he became aware of the need for a workbase which would be more substantial than the traditional sawhorse but at the same time portable. The solution, an embryo *Workmate*, was essentially a small, low workbench with a conventional vice. The top was constructed from two pieces of timber, the gap between them prompting the concept of the integral vice. In 1967 Hickman left Lotus to pursue his own design work, which was to include two successful chair projects – a fibreglass deckchair and seating for the lounges in the Q.E.2. During this time he had also been working on the *Workmate*, which, having been rejected by Britain's major tool companies, he initially marketed himself.

The *Workmate Mk I* was characterized by two features which distinguished it from an ordinary small-scale workbench: because it folded flat, not only was it portable but it was also easily storable when not in use. Sold initially through exhibitions and direct order, the market need for this device was soon proved, with some 25,000 being sold in the first three years, not only to the growing number of do-it-yourself enthusiasts but also to industry and to educational and Government establishments.

Although the height had been determined by that of the traditional sawhorse, an optional accessory, the *Team-mate*, which clamped over the *Workmate*, brought the working surface up to conventional bench height. This cumbersome arrangement was overcome with the *Mk II* model, which could be adjusted to either height, and which employed a sophisticated structure allowing for rigidity irrespective of the variety of stress loads (downwards in the case of hammering, for instance, front to rear when sawing was taking place, or sideways during planing) which the *Workmate* would be subjected to in the course of its various functions.

Other improvements included the development of the vice/worktop into a multi-purpose tool in its own right, capable of holding round or irregularly-shaped objects, as well as providing fixing points for power tools.

In 1971 Black and Decker UK (which, together with several other companies, had originally rejected the *Workmate* and subsequently tried to obtain the now obviously valuable manufacturing and marketing rights) succeeded in obtaining the European licencing rights, officially introducing the *Mk II* the following year. America remained sceptical, with Black and Decker, Sears Roebuck and Stanley still rejecting it. Even so, by 1976 a million *Workmates* had been sold, and alongside this commercial recognition, it was also picking up design kudos, including, ironically, being selected by the US Patent Office for the Bicentennial Exhibition.

Now, with many millions of *Workmates* in use throughout the world, it has become an indispensable tool for many trades and hobbies ■

THE WURLITZER 1015

Paul Fuller 1946

Dispassionate analysis leads to the inevitable conclusion that the famous 1946 *Wurlitzer* jukebox is not 'good' design according to most accepted criteria. In many ways it is no more than a commercial pastiche of pre-war designs put together to capitalize on the initial euphoria of post-war production. The work of Paul Fuller, who was responsible for the glamorous style which is synonymous with Wurlitzer, the *Model 1015* combines all the decorative elements which characterize his work: changing coloured lights, fancy metalwork, bubble tubes and moulded wood casework. Yet it is essentially archaic, and even mechanically had nothing new to offer. Yet paradoxically, whilst a contemporary market rival, the *Aerion*, should have been, in theory, the superior product, being designed by Raymond Loewy and representing post-war state-of-the-art technology, it is the *Wurlitzer* which remains the definitive jukebox. Unlike Loewy's design, the *Wurlitzer* achieved a charismatic quality whereby the total adds up to more than the sum of its parts, and so it represents a form of intuitive industrial folk art ■

The 1946 *Wurlitzer 1015* is seen as the archetypal jukebox, a thing of flamboyant excess which still has sufficient impact for Wurlitzer to have reintroduced it for commercial use, both as a conventional disc player and in a CD version.

THE ZIPPO

George Grant
Blaisdell 1932

Although the overriding popular impression of 20th century American product design is that of ephemeral trends, an image largely based on the fifties doctrine of planned obsolescence but also owing much to its seemingly constant quest for novelty, there is nevertheless a strong practical, even puritanical streak — a reflection of that element in the national character which, from the early settlers onwards, valued the integrity of solid workmanship and engineering.

For the Zippo Manufacturing Company of Pennsylvania the throw-away society is anathema, for they have never broken their promise that 'any *Zippo* lighter, when returned to our factory, will be put in first class mechanical condition free of charge. We have never charged a cent for the repair of a *Zippo* regardless of its age or condition.' This is even more remarkable since the *Zippo* is no expensive, luxury item (and now even Rolex will refuse to repair one of their watches when it reaches a certain age, let alone for free) but rather a low-price, utility object. Nor have Zippo, their lighters guaranteed functional immortality, turned to styling obsolescence to boost sales, for although the *Zippo* has appeared with a great variety of decorative embellishments, in essence it has not changed since 1937.

The history of the *Zippo* is as simple as the lighter itself. The inventor, George Grant Blaisdell, had been shown an Austrian lighter which, though robust, was awkward to operate. Nevertheless, the user defended it with the factual observation, 'It works'. Blaisdell, recognizing infallible reliability to be the key, redesigned the Austrian lighter, housing it in a simple brass case and shielding the wick with an enlarged chimney, making it windproof. A large knurled wheel to operate the flint ensures that, provided the lighter is raised with the prescribed upwards movement to free any airlock, it always lights on the first flick. The *Zippo* (named for, as Blaisdell described it, its snappy sound) went onto the market in 1932. In 1937 it was restyled to its present form, the case becoming shorter and losing its sharp corners to give it a more rounded look; the lid hinge, instead of being simply riveted on, became concealed. Despite a pervading whiff of lighter fuel which emanates from it when used, and despite its lack of sophistication (the flame cannot be adjusted, and is only extinguished by closing the lid) it remains, at least in its unembellished form, an example of timeless functionalism ■

The original *Zippo*, shown here, required only minor restyling to produce the lighter which has defied any concepts of product obsolescence to become part of consumer folklore.

■ INDEX